MRS. BOONE'S

MRS. BOONE'S
Favorite Early-American Recipes

Compiled by Franklin Fox

Momentum Books, Ltd.

Troy, Michigan

Manufactured in the United States of America

2000   1999   1998   3   2   1

Momentum Books, Ltd.
6964 Crooks Road, Suite 1
Troy, Michigan 48098

Library of Congress Cataloging-in-Publication Data

Fox, Franklin, 1935-
    Mrs.Boone's favorite early-American recipes / compiled by
  Franklin Fox,
        p.   cm.
      ISBN 1-879094-56-8 (alk. paper)
      1.   Cookery, American.   I. Title
  TX715.F796   1998
  641.5973 --dc21

Introduction   **ix**

Ingredients   x
Measurements   x
Equivalents   xi
Times and Temperatures   xi
Advice on Soup   xii
Advice on Meats   xiii
Cooking Methods   xiv
Rendering Lard   xvi
Keeping Cured Meat   xvi
Advice on Cake   xvii

Breads & Fritters

Breakfast Puffs   2
Fried Bread   2
Kentucky Corn Bread   3
Johnnycake   4
Steamed Corn Bread   4
Corn Pone   5
Corn Dodger   6
Western Corn Bread   6
Hush Puppies   7
Fritters   8
Corn Fritters   8

Bell Fritters   9
Apple Fritters   10
Potato Fritters   11
Tomato Fritters   11
Notions   12

Soups

Bean Soup   14
Beef Tea   14
Black Bean Soup   15
Cabbage Soup   16
Clam Soup   17
Corn Soup   18
Fish Soup   19
Okra Soup   20
Ox Tail Soup   21
Oyster Soup   22
Oyster Stew   22
Green Pea Soup   23
Quick & Easy Green Pea   24
Tomato Soup   25
Easy Cream of Tomato   25
Vegetable Soup   26
Gumbo   27
Creole Gumbo   28

Meats

Beef Omelet   30
Corned Beef   31
Easy Corned Beef   32
Fricasseed Beef   32
Frizzled Beef   33
Pressed Beef   34
Savory Beef   34
Roly Poly   35
Boiled Dinner   36
Deviled Meat   37
Boiled Ham   38
Ham with Madeira   39
Virginia Ham   40
Stewed Kidneys   41
Potato Crust   42
Pig's Feet   42
Stewed Ox Tail   43
Cured Pork   44
Beef Stew   45
Veal Olives   46
Fricandeau of Veal   47

Poultry

Virginia Fried Chicken	50
Boiled Chicken	50
Fricassee of Chicken	51
Goose Giblet Pie	52
Roast Goose	54
Roast Turkey	55
Turkey Giblet Gravy	56
Roast Turkey with Oyster Dressing	56
Roast Turkey with Chestnuts	57

Wild Game

Roast Canvasback Duck	60
Guinea-Fowl	61
Plover	62
Partridge	63
Partridge Pie	64
Pheasant	65
Broiled Pigeons	66
Stewed Pigeons	67
Possum	68
Prairie Chicken	68
Quail on Toast	69
Quail Pie	70
Reed Birds	71
Snow Birds	71
Fried Rabbit	72
Roast Rabbit	73
Stewed Rabbit	74
Broiled Squirrel	75
Squirrel Pie	75
Wild Turkey	76
Terrapin Stew	77
Venison Steak	78
Haunch of Venison	79
Wine Sauce for Roast Game	80

Fish

Baked Fish	82
Boiled Fish	83
Stewed Fish	83
Fish Balls	84
Fried Perch	84
Fried Smelts	85
Salt Codfish	86
Codfish Balls	86
Baked Cod	87

Vegetables & Side Dishes

Boiled Cabbage with Bacon	90
Spiced Cabbage	90
Cabbage Salad	91
Hot Slaw	92
Warm Slaw	92
Stewed Celery	93
Roast Chestnuts	93
Cheese Straws	94
Tomato Chowchow	95
Corn Pudding	96
Corn Oysters	96
Cucumbers	97
Fried Cucumbers	97
Eggs as a Side-Dish	98
Eggs with Fried Potatoes	98
Baked Eggs	99
Snow Eggs	99
Hominy	100
Hominy Grits	100
Okra	101
Parsnips	101
Boiled Onions	102
Baked Onions	103
Piccalilli	104

Pickles	105	Barbecue Sauce	125	**Cakes, Pies & Desserts**	
Quick Pickles	106	Bread Sauce	126		
Indian Pickles	107	Butter Sauce	127	Bachelor's Pudding	146
Sweet Pickles	108	Drawn Butter Sauce	127	Brown Betty	147
Pigs in Blankets	109	Cabbage Dressing	128	Cake	148
Yorkshire Pudding	109	Celery Dressing	128	Cake Frosting	149
Boiled Potatoes	110	Catsup	129	Christmas Cake	150
Kentucky Potatoes	111	Celery Sauce	130	Coffee Cake	150
Potato Cakes	112	Chili Sauce	131	Cookies	151
Potato Pudding	112	Cold Meat Sauce	132	Delicate Cake	152
Potato Dumplings	113	Egg Sauce	133	Drop Cakes	153
Quirled Potatoes	114	Gherkin Sauce	133	Drop Johnnies	154
Saratoga Potatoes	114	Horseradish Sauce	134	Eve's Pudding	155
Sauerkraut	115	Lemon Sauce	135	Fried Cakes	156
Salsify	116	Simple Mayonnaise	136	Homely Pie	157
Broiled Tomatoes	117	Mint Sauce	137	Lady Fingers	158
Fried Tomatoes	117	Mushroom Sauce	137	Lemon Pie without Lemon	159
Turnips	118	Mustard	138	Mincemeat for Pies	160
Pork and Turnips	118	Onion Sauce	139	Moonshine	161
Russian Salad	119	Parsley Sauce	139	Pork Cake	162
Herring Salad	120	Raspberry Vinegar	140	Pound Cake	163
Veal Salad	121	Tomato Sauce	141	Potato Pie	164
		White Sauce	142	Peach Pie	164
Sauces & Dressings		Wine Sauce for Meat	142	Quaker Pudding	165
		Worcestershire Sauce	143	Raisin Pie	166
Aspic Jelly	124			Rhubarb Pie	167

Soda Cakes	168	Pink Cream	185	Tomato Beer	204
Shortcake	169	Lemon Cream	186	Lemonade	205
Strawberry Shortcake	169	Orange Cream	187	Linseed Tea	206
Fancy Strawberry		Russian Cream	188	Chamomile Tea	206
Shortcake	170	Velvet Cream	189	Elderberry Wine	207
Snow Custard	171	Walnut Cream	190	Unfermented Wine	208
Sponge Cake	172	Whipped Cream	191		
Sour Cream Pie	173	Boiled Custard	192		
Syllabub	173	A Grand Trifle	193		
Steamed Pudding	174	Ice Cream	194		
Suet Pudding	175	Pure Ice Cream	194		
Tea Cake	176	Coffee Ice Cream	195		
Widow's Cake	177	Tea Ice Cream	195		
		Lemon Ice	196		

Sweets & Such

		Water Ice	196	
Bisque	180	Peaches & Cream	197	
Candied Fruit	180	Cherry Syrup	197	
Molasses Candy	181	Lemon Sherbet	198	
Molasses Pull Candy	181	Milk Sherbet	198	
Sugar Candy	182	Fried Plantains	199	
Chocolate Caramels	183	Baked Plantains	199	
Fudge	183			
Apple Cream	184	**Beverages**		
Chocolate Cream	184			
Coffee Cream	185	Spruce Beer	202	
		Cream Beer	203	

Introduction

As our country matured, our tastes grew more refined. We set aside the basics in favor of the new, the fashionable and the exotic. We became sophisticated and enlightened, and our raw nation grew into a world power. Unfortunately, much was lost in the transition. We tended to forget the strength that resides in simplicity, and the joy of the unpretentious life.

This is a collection of recipes that have been lost in time. Yet they yield those basic foods from which our forebears gathered strength to tame this magnificent land. They require only the most basic cooking skills, and the few fundamental ingredients and utensils found in any pioneer's log cabin or sod hut. And the foods are as rich in flavor as they are in history.

Merely perusing these receipts (as they used to be called) is in itself a nostalgic journey into our past. But nothing quite equals the actual cooking and tasting of these zesty dishes. I hope you will try at least some of them, and share the enjoyment with your friends.

Mrs. B.

Ingredients

Modern ingredients such as skim milk, artificial sweeteners and fat-free sour cream may seriously compromise the results and are probably not worth the salt. However, vegetable shortening may be safely substituted for lard, which is why it was invented in the first place. But there is nothing quite like the original. Ask any cook who insists on lard for the ultimate in a flaky pie crust.

Measurements

Rather than specific measured amounts, cooks of yore were accustomed to using "a pinch," "a piece," or "some." As a result, the end-product usually varied according to the caprice of the cook or the scarcity of an ingredient. Experience used to be the best teacher. It still is.

Equivalents

Today's recipes rely on the eight-ounce cup as the standard quantity. Recipes from the turn of the century and earlier called for "teacups," "pints," and "gills." A pint was always a pint or sixteen ounces, but a teacup and a gill were both equal to four ounces. In this book I have made the appropriate adjustment.

Cooking Times and Temperatures

Bygone ovens were not equipped with thermometers and thermostats. The savvy cook judged baking temperatures by opening the oven door and quickly waving a hand through it, or by sprinkling a little dry flour inside. If the flour turned dark, the oven was considered too hot and allowed to cool.

Baking times used to be based on experience and a sharp eye that could tell doneness by color and smell, or by gently probing with a fork or toothpick.

Some sage advice from olden days on cooking soup.

❧ To make good soup, properly flavored and palatable, requires much practice.

❧The best foundation for soup is lean uncooked meat. A quart of water to a pound of meat is the usual quantity. When soup is made from fresh meat, it should always cook in cold water.

❧Grease should always be skimmed from all soups, and slow boiling is very important in order to extract the strength from the meat. When meat is boiled very fast over a hot fire it retains its juice and becomes tough and hard.

❧Beef is more generally used as soup meat. To this may be added mutton and veal bones broken up. Also, bits of chicken, turkey and ham make a well-flavored soup, much better than any one meat.

❧A soup pot should always be kept on hand for soups, into which bits of meat, bones from a rib roast, gravies left from roast meats, and all fragments may be thrown. Put on the fire and cook until done. Strain and put in an earthen vessel for use.

❧If kept in a cold place, the soup will be good for several days. Remove all fat that may rise. Vegetables should not be cooked in stock as they will cause it to sour.

More "meaty" words to the wise from out of our past.

❧In selecting beef, choose that of a fine grain—smooth, bright red color and white fat. The sixth, seventh and eighth ribs are the choicest cuts for roasting. The bones must be removed and the meat rolled. Use the bones for soup.

❧Veal, when fresh, is firm and dry. Joints are stiff and kidneys are covered with fat.

❧The flesh of good mutton is of dark red, with fat firm and white. Lamb, when fresh, is pale red. If the neck veins are not of a bluish tint, the meat is not good. When roasted, the meat should be covered with the caul [*fat from the cavity*] as the fat that drips from that in roasting preserves the moisture of the meat.

❧Pork and veal should be well cooked. If the meat of pork is young, the lean will break on being pinched. The skin will be smooth and thin. If kernels should be found in the fat, reject the meat.

❧When necessary to wash meats, it should be done as hurriedly as possible, as the water extracts the juices. Beef, when just cut from a quarter, should not be washed. It is only necessary to wipe it with a clean dry cloth.

❧When meat is frozen, it should be put in cold water to thaw and cooked as soon as possible or it will lose its sweetness.

Cooking methods that helped build a strong and healthy nation.

❧Roasting meat before a fire is undoubtedly superior but very few families have the facilities. The cook stove is becoming supreme and no person will object to a joint or a bird nicely roasted in an oven. In order to retain the juices and flavor of the meat, cover the surface of the roast with a rich glaze. Put it into a hot oven so that as the gravy exudes, it congeals on the outside, thus confining or sealing up the pores. If the meat is lean, a small quantity of water must be added. If it is fat, the water should be omitted entirely. Meat should be turned so that it may brown equally.

When done, carefully pour off all the fat from the pan. The thick sediment in the bottom of the pan will make sufficient gravy by adding a little boiling water. No flour is needed to thicken the gravy. Merely place the pan on the stove and boil for two or three minutes. It is a better plan to add neither salt nor pepper to the meat before cooking, as salt draws out the gravy which it is your purpose to keep in. Pepper, when used on the surface of meats, becomes parched and leaves a bad taste.

❧Larding moistens meat while cooking and adds richness to its flavor. To lard meat is simply to introduce into the surface of the flesh the clear fat of pork or bacon. This is done by cutting the fat into thin strips about two inches long and not quite half an inch thick. The strips are placed into the cleft of a larding needle and drawn through the meat, leaving half an inch or so on each side of the stitch. The whole surface may be arranged in rows, or any fanciful forms desired.

In frying meat, failure is always very apparent. There are two very important rules to observe. Firstly, your fat must be boiling hot. Secondly, any crumbs should be thoroughly rolled and finely sifted.

A deep enameled or iron pan should be used, with sufficient fat to cover the meat thoroughly. It is best to be very generous with the fat as it is quite as economical to use more as it is to use less. The fat can be used again if strained and put aside in a clean vessel.

Good judgment and close attention are very necessary in order to boil meat right. Meat should be boiled very slowly over a slow fire to concentrate its juices. It is proper to keep the pot gently boiling, but the boiling should never cease. If so, the meat will absorb the water and cause it to be flat and insipid. The more gently meat boils the more tender it will be. If boiled too hard, the meat is toughened and juices extracted.

Remove the scum when it first begins to boil, and replenish with boiling water to keep the meat covered. To every pound of fresh meat allow fifteen minutes to boil, and to salted meat allow twenty minutes.

Stewing is the basis of all made dishes, and a most economical and savory manner of cooking. A hearty stew should never be greasy. Nor should it be very highly seasoned. Its perfection depends upon the slowness with which it is done.

A stew should never boil nor even simmer. Hence it is most safely performed by placing the stewing pan in another vessel of water. The pot lid should be kept closed. An occasional shaking of the contents will save stirring.

Broiling is a simple mode of cooking that requires little care and attention. A brisk, clear fire is essential. If the fire should be too heavy, the gridiron may be raised in order that the meat may not scorch.

The gridiron must be very hot before the meat is placed upon it. If allowed to remain without turning until the gravy stands on top, when turned the gravy is lost in the fire. But when turned quickly and at the proper time, the meat is sealed at once and the gravy retained.

Any pork fat may be used to render lard but leaf fat is best and produces the highest quality lard. Leaf fat is found lining the abdominal cavities of hogs and enclosing their kidneys. Fat of the backbone is also very nice. But if you use fat from the entrails it must be washed well and soaked for several days in salted water to draw out the impurities, changing the water often.

Cut the fat into small pieces and boil rapidly. When the cracklings begin to brown, move the pot to a slower fire to prevent burning. When all the fat has been rendered, allow the pot to cool. The lard will rise to the top and congeal so it can be skimmed off in chunks. Cracklings of leaf lard will be light brown when sufficiently cooked and sink to the bottom of the pot. They may be used for making soap.

To keep cured meat cover the bottom of a wooden box with a layer of field corn. Put in a layer of cured meat and another layer of corn, alternating until the meat is used up. Make sure the top layer is corn and that it's quite thick. After the meat has been consumed, the corn can be used for fattening hogs.

Some thoughts of old on cake.

❧Some people begrudge their families cake on the ground that it is expensive. This is a mistake. Milk, eggs, butter, flour and sugar are the ingredients of most cakes. The first three all farmers have or should have plenty of, and sugar is no longer costly.

❧As a condensed food, cake is cheaper than the best beefsteak, even in the country, and more than twice as nourishing. Eggs are more nourishing, pound for pound, than fresh meat. A quart of good milk contains as much nourishment as a pound of fresh beef.

❧Ingredients must be of the best, for the best are most economical. Never allow butter to get oily before mixing it in a cake. Always use an earthen or enameled dish to work the ingredients. Tin, if not new, is apt to discolor the batter. Egg will tarnish even silver, hence always use a clean wooden spoon.

For small cakes the oven should be fairly hot, and for larger cakes only moderately so. If a broom-straw is pushed through the thick part of the cake and comes out clean and free from dough, the cake is done. When you take the cake from the oven, do not remove it from the pan until somewhat cool and certainly no sooner than fifteen minutes.

BREADS & FRITTERS

BREAKFAST PUFFS

butter
2 eggs
2 cups milk

salt
3 cups flour

Butter the cups into which the batter is to be poured.

Beat the eggs and stir in the milk. Add a pinch of salt and some melted butter. Pour all into the flour so as not to have it lumpy. Stir thoroughly and fill baking cups two-thirds full. Bake until done.

FRIED BREAD

Very likely the genesis of French toast. —Mrs. B.

dried bread
lard
butter

eggs
cream
(gravy)

Cut the dry bread into slices, dip in water and fry in hot lard and butter or gravy and butter. When nicely browned, cover with sweet cream and well-beaten eggs. Fry to the bread and serve hot.

KENTUCKY CORN BREAD

3 cups cornmeal
2 cups buttermilk
1 egg
teaspoon baking soda
teaspoon salt
tablespoon lard or butter

Mix ingredients thoroughly and bake in a quick oven.

Early settlers learned about cornmeal from Native American Indians who made it by grinding up dried field corn. Note the omission of sugar, probably because it was too scarce to needlessly sweeten a country favorite. —Mrs. B.

JOHNNYCAKE

2 ½ cups cornmeal   1 teaspoon salt
2 ¼ cups milk   1 egg

Beat the egg and combine with cornmeal, salt and milk. Continue to beat until blended.
Drop spoonfuls onto a well-greased skillet and fry on both sides until golden
brown.

This basic corn bread was taken on the trail and originally called journey cake. —Mrs. B.

STEAMED CORN BREAD

2 cups cornmeal   pinch of salt
1 cup flour   ½ teaspoon baking soda
1 ½ cups milk   1 tablespoon molasses

Make a thick batter of the ingredients and place in a basin. Put the basin on a rack in a
kettle of boiling water. Cover and steam for 1½ hours.

CORN PONE

2½ cups cornmeal
1 cup graham flour
½ cup molasses
2 teaspoons baking soda
1 quart buttermilk

Mix ingredients thoroughly and pour into a buttered tin or porcelain kettle. Cover securely and place in larger kettle so it will be submerged. Fill with boiling water and boil hard for six hours.

Slip from the kettle and into a pan. Bake slowly for two hours.

This is corn bread made without eggs but with plenty of stamina. No, cooking times are not in error. In olden days most of the heat in the house came from the kitchen. Hence, you might want to wait for a cold day before giving this a try. —Mrs. B.

CORN DODGER

scant quart of cornmeal
½ teaspoon salt

2 cups buttermilk
1 teaspoon baking soda

Mix well and bake in a moderately heated oven.

Corn bread that's either fried, baked, or boiled as a dumpling. —Mrs. B.

WESTERN CORN BREAD

2 cups cornmeal
1 tablespoon salt
¾ cup brown sugar

flour
½ cup lively yeast
(molasses)

Pour boiling water into cornmeal and stir until about as thick as griddle-cake batter. Add salt, brown sugar or molasses. Stir in some flour until the mixture gets quite stiff. Add yeast when cool. Place in a warm place to rise.

When partially risen, sprinkle with flour and gently mold into a loaf. When the loaf fills the basin, bake in a moderate oven for two hours.

HUSH PUPPIES

2 cups cornmeal
1 teaspoon baking soda
1 teaspoon salt
1 cup buttermilk
1 egg
1 small onion, finely chopped
lard

Combine cornmeal, baking soda and salt. Add buttermilk and egg, and beat until smooth. Stir in the chopped onion.

Drop spoonfuls of the mixture into hot lard and fry until golden brown.

FRITTERS

Fritters are different from pancakes in that they require less liquid and more eggs. When making fritters, use haste, but beat the batter thoroughly and cook at once.

2 eggs	**lard**
2 cups milk	**pinch of salt**
1 teaspoon cream of tartar (or baking powder)	**½ teaspoon baking soda**

Beat eggs, stir in remaining ingredients and beat thoroughly. Drop spoonfuls of batter into hot lard and fry until brown.

To remove the brown residue from the lard, drop in a crust of bread to soak it up.

CORN FRITTERS

6 ears of corn	**salt and pepper**
1 tablespoon flour	**lard**
2 eggs	

Grate the corn and combine the kernels with flour, eggs and salt and pepper. Drop spoonfuls of the mixture into hot lard and fry until golden brown.

BELL FRITTERS

6 eggs
1 tablespoon butter
2 cups flour
lard

Beat the eggs well and set them aside.

Boil two cups of water and add the butter.

In a separate bowl, make a paste by adding cold water to the flour. Pour the boiling water over the paste a little at a time to keep it smooth. Return to the kettle and stir carefully to prevent lumping.

Add to the eggs a spoonful at a time until well blended, beating rapidly all the while so the eggs do not cook in lumps.

Continue to beat until batter is light. Then form fritters on a spoon in the shape of an egg and drop into boiling hot lard. Fry until golden brown and serve with molasses or maple syrup.

APPLE FRITTERS

6 tart apples, not too mellow
3 eggs
2 cups milk
pinch of baking soda
pinch of salt
flour
sugar
cinnamon
lard
powdered sugar

Pare and core the apples, and cut them into round slices about ½-inch thick. Beat the eggs lightly and add in the milk. Add baking soda, salt and just enough flour to make a stiff batter.

Dip apple slices in a mixture of sugar and cinnamon. Put each slice on the forefinger and whirl it in batter until thickly covered. Drop into hot lard or drippings and fry until golden brown.

Dust with powdered sugar before serving.

POTATO FRITTERS

6 boiled potatoes   **3 eggs**
2 cups sweet cream or milk **pinch of salt**
flour   **butter**

Separate eggs and beat the whites. Grate the cold potatoes and pour in cream. Add enough flour to make the batter stiff. Add egg yolks, beaten whites and salt. Fry in hot butter.

TOMATO FRITTERS

This recipe is so simple a child can do it, but it makes a delicious breakfast dish. —Mrs. B.

tomatoes   **cracker crumbs**
eggs   **butter**

Leave the skins on the tomatoes because they will hold the meat together. Cut tomatoes into thick slices and dip in beaten egg and cracker crumbs. Fry in hot butter.

NOTIONS

2 cups flour
milk
¼ teaspoon salt
2 ounces butter

Make the flour into a soft dough that can be rolled by adding milk, salt and butter. Roll into large round cakes of wafer-like thickness and stick well with a fork.

Bake but do not brown, and remove while crisp and still white.

Otherwise known as thin biscuits. —Mrs. B.

SOUPS

BEAN SOUP

3 cups beans   **lemon slices**
medium onion   **black pepper**
1 lb. salt pork

Soak the beans overnight. Add salt pork, about four quarts of water and boil slowly for at least three hours. Season with pepper and strain.

Serve with slices of lemon.

BEEF TEA

A weak broth not quite the same as beef bouillon, which is rich broth seasoned with herbs and vegetables.

1 lb. chopped beef   **1 quart water**

Simmer in a covered saucepan until water has been reduced to two cups. Strain and let cool.

Skim off the fat and serve hot or cold.

BLACK BEAN SOUP

2 quarts black beans
corned beef
black pepper
ground cloves
hard-boiled eggs
wine

Soak the beans overnight.

Boil the beans until they start to soften. Add enough corned beef to salt the soup and continue boiling until beans are quite soft. Strain and return the liquid to the soup kettle. If too thick, add warm water. Season with pepper and cloves, and flavor with any kind of wine. (The soup is very good without wine.)

Before serving, add some finely chopped egg to each bowl.

Soups

CABBAGE SOUP

This splendid cool-weather soup takes about an hour and a half to prepare and serves eight.

2 quarts stock
1 large cabbage
3 carrots
2 medium onions
5 slices lean bacon
salt
black pepper

Scald the cabbage, and cut and drain it.

Line the bottom of a stewing pan with bacon and add the cabbage, carrots and onions. Moisten with stock and simmer until cabbage is tender. Add rest of the stock and cook gently for one-half hour.

Skim off all fat, season with salt and pepper and serve.

16

CLAM SOUP

2 dozen clams   **flour**
2 cups milk   **3 eggs**
butter

Chop the clams fine. Stew for one hour in their own liquor with an additional two quarts of water. Strain and put over the fire. As soon as it boils, add the milk and thicken with butter the size of an egg mixed well with flour.

Beat the eggs lightly and pour them into a soup tureen. Carefully stir in the hot soup.

CORN SOUP

8 large ears of corn
2 quarts milk
2 tablespoons butter
1 tablespoon flour

3 egg yolks
salt
black pepper

Scrape the kernels off the cobs, cover with water and boil until perfectly done. Add milk and bring to a boil.

Roll the butter in flour and stir it into the soup. Let boil for ten minutes. Pour over beaten egg yolks, stirring briskly all the while. Season with salt and pepper and serve immediately.

FISH SOUP

any firm-fleshed fish
1 quart fish or chicken stock
a handful of parsley
a piece of celery
1 onion stuck with 2 cloves
a blade of mace
black pepper
salt

Skin and fillet the fish, and cut it into small pieces. Put the head, bones and trimmings into a saucepan with the stock. Add parsley, celery, onion and mace. Salt and pepper to taste. Simmer for three or four hours. Skim, strain and return the liquid to the soup kettle. Bring to a boil and add the fish.

When the fish is cooked, take out the pieces and put them into a soup tureen with a little chopped and blanched parsley. Strain the soup into the tureen and serve at once.

OKRA SOUP

8 cups okra	**sweet cream**
2 chickens	**cooked rice**
3 strips of bacon (or ¼ lb. ham)	**cayenne pepper**
4 cups tomatoes	**black pepper**
2 onions	**salt**

Cook the okra separately in a saucepan. Fry the chicken, bacon and onions in a skillet. When done, add water and rinse everything into a soup kettle with plenty of water. Put in the tomatoes and let it simmer.

When the chicken is tender enough for the meat to be pulled from the bone, strain through a colander. Return the bacon (or ham) and tomatoes to the soup.

Pull the chicken meat off its bones and add to the soup along with the cooked okra. Simmer until suitably thick. Season with salt, pepper and cayenne.

Put some cooked rice in each serving dish, add a little sweet cream and ladle on the soup. Alternately, the rice and cream may be added to the soup itself.

You'll need a mighty big pot for this soup, and an even mightier appetite. —Mrs. B.

OX TAIL SOUP

3 skinned ox tails
butter
2 to 4 onions
1 carrot
1 turnip
1 head of celery
salt
black pepper
allspice

In olden days, nothing was wasted, not even tails from oxen. Question is, where can you find ox tails today? —Mrs. B.

The day before, cut the ox tails into pieces, remove the fat and brown them in butter.

Next day, skim off the grease and boil the ox tails in about three quarts of water. Add onions, carrot, turnip and celery. Salt and pepper to taste along with a good shake of allspice.

Boil four to five hours. Lift out the meat and strain the soup. Choose the best meat, return it to the soup and serve.

OYSTER SOUP

1 quart oysters　　　　　　**1 tablespoon butter**
1 quart milk　　　　　　　　**salt**
cracker dust or flour　　　　**black pepper**

Add the oyster liquid to the milk and bring to a boil. Use cracker dust or flour to thicken.

Add butter, put in the oysters, and season with salt and pepper. Serve right away.

OYSTER STEW

Simple, quick and delicious.

6 cups oysters　　　　　　　**salt**
½ gallon milk　　　　　　　**butter**

Boil the liquid from the oysters in a saucepan and skim. Add the milk, and when that boils, add the oysters.

When the oysters begin to curl, remove them from the fire and salt to taste. Add butter in generous quantity and serve hot.

GREEN PEA SOUP

½ peck of fresh green peas [*4 quarts*]
1 onion
thyme
parsley
salt
black pepper
½ teaspoon flour

Boil the peas in six quarts of water until done. Strain out the peas, press them through a sieve and return them to the pot.

Fry a finely chopped onion in a little lard, not too brown. Add to the soup along with chopped thyme and parsley. Salt and pepper to taste. Stir flour into the boiling soup to thicken and serve with cubes of toasted bread.

QUICK & EASY GREEN PEA SOUP

1 can of peas
salt
1 tablespoon butter
2 tablespoons flour
2 cups milk
2 cups water
tabasco sauce

Pour off the liquid from a can of peas and put the peas in pot with enough fresh water to cover. Season with salt, cook for a few minutes and mash the peas through a fine sieve.

Melt the butter in a soup kettle, add the flour and cook until frothy. Only then add milk and water and season with tabasco, salt and pepper. Boil for about a minute and add sieved peas. Boil for another minute and serve.

TOMATO SOUP

4 cups ripe tomatoes	**butter**
2 cups water	**salt**
1 teaspoon baking soda	**black pepper**
4 cups milk	**flour**

Put the tomatoes into the water and boil them for about twenty minutes. Add *baking soda*, milk and a piece of butter the size of an egg. Salt and pepper to taste.

Thicken with a little flour and strain before serving.

EASY CREAM OF TOMATO SOUP

2 cups white sauce	**1 teaspoon butter**
4 cups tomato juice	**paprika**

Heat white sauce and add tomato juice. Add butter and seasoning.

Serve hot with croutons or saltines.

VEGETABLE SOUP

1 beef shank
turnips
carrots
peeled tomatoes
¼ lb. green corn grated off the cob

¼ lb. potatoes
onions
young okra
black pepper
salt

Crush the bone in the shank and cover the shank with cold water. Bring to a boil and skim. Add sliced turnips and carrots. Cook for four hours so the liquid is reduced to about two quarts for every three to four pounds of meat.

When the soup is half done, add one cup of tomatoes for each two quarts of soup. One hour later, add some sliced okra in the same proportion. Half an hour before serving, add sliced potatoes and corn. Lightly flavor with chopped onions, and season with salt and pepper.

If okra or tomatoes cannot be had, thicken the soup with a little flour and cooked rice.

This is the soup that was most commonly made in this country. —Mrs. B.

GUMBO

2 good-size chickens
flour
butter
salt
6 cups oysters
ham
2 teaspoons powdered sassafras leaves
black pepper

Cut up chickens. Flour and fry in butter until light brown. Put the chicken in a soup kettle, add three quarts hot water and simmer slowly for two hours. Braid a little flour and butter together for thickening and add to the soup. Salt to taste.

Strain oysters and add juice to the soup along with a few slices of cold ham. Boil gently for ten to twelve minutes. Just before removing soup from the fire, stir in the sassafras, simmer a few minutes and add the oysters. Season with pepper and serve in a deep dish. Garnish with cooked rice.

CREOLE GUMBO

butter or lard
bacon
okra
crab
shrimp
ham

Put a lump of butter or lard in a saucepan along with a few small pieces of finely chopped bacon. Brown the bacon and add some finely sliced okra. Add some hot water little by little, stirring constantly.

To this brew add finely cut crab and shrimp, plus a small piece of ham.

Serve with cooked rice.

This is typical of old-time recipes in that it does not stoop to specify amounts. Details like that are left to the good sense of the cook. —Mrs. B.

MEATS

BEEF OMELET

3 eggs
3 lbs. of thin beefsteak
1 light lb. suet
salt
black pepper
a little sage
7 crackers

Break the eggs onto the beefsteak. Sprinkle with finely chopped suet, seasoning and crackers rolled fine. Turn the meat into a roll and bake.

If you have any doubt that our forebears were hearty eaters—and totally oblivious to the risks of cholesterol—this "omelet" should dispel those doubts. —Mrs. B.

CORNED BEEF

50 lbs. beef
3 lbs. salt
1 lb. brown sugar
1 ounce saltpeter
2 ounces baking soda
½ ounce red pepper

Enough to feed a famished troop of cavalry! —Mrs. B.

Dissolve the corning ingredients in water. Pack the beef closely in a barrel and cover with the mixture. Let stand a week, longer if weather is cool.

Pour the brine off into a kettle. Boil and carefully skim it, then let it cool and pour it back over the beef.

The meat will keep for a very long time.

EASY CORNED BEEF

10-lb. beef roast
2 ½ cups salt

Cover the roast with cold water, add salt and cook until tender. Any less salt will diminish the goodness.

Good when hot, better when pressed and served cold.

FRICASSEED BEEF

beef from the forequarter [*chuck or shoulder*]   **black pepper**
2 tablespoons flour   **salt**

Cover the beef with water and cook until tender. When half done, season with salt and pepper. If the water does not boil away soon enough, pour it off and let the beef fry for ten minutes.

For gravy, mix some flour into the beef fat and pour it over the meat.

FRIZZLED BEEF

1 lb. beef
butter
2 eggs
3 tablespoons cream
flour
parsley
salt
black pepper

Frizzle happens to be a contraction of fry and sizzle. Any further explanation would be superfluous. —Mrs. B.

Shave the beef into very thin slices and place the slices in a hot skillet. Pour in a little warm water, stir briefly and drain. Add a piece of butter the size of an egg.

Beat the eggs with cream, dredge [*coat heavily*] with flour and pour it over beef. Season with parsley, salt and pepper.

PRESSED BEEF

beef brisket	**saltpeter**
salt	**tomato sauce**

Cure the meat by coating it with salt and pulverized saltpeter and letting it rest for five or six days. Cold will slow the process significantly.

Boil slowly until tender. Press until perfectly cold. Slice thin and serve with tomato sauce.

SAVORY BEEF

3 ½ lbs. ground round	**milk**
3 eggs	**nutmeg**
20 oyster crackers, rolled fine	**black pepper**
4 tablespoons sweet cream	**salt**
butter	

Combine the meat, eggs, crackers, cream and butter the size of an egg. While mixing, salt and pepper to taste and add a little nutmeg. Thin with milk to the consistency of biscuit dough. Place in a buttered pan and bake for 1½ hours. When cold, slice and serve with tea or for lunch.

ROLY POLY

1 round steak
mashed potatoes
bread crumbs
butter
parsley
onion
salt
black pepper
cracker crumbs

Beat the steak thoroughly and lay it flat on a cutting board.

Make a dressing from mashed potatoes, bread crumbs, a small piece of butter, some minced parsley and chopped onion. Season with salt and pepper.

Spread the dressing on the steak and roll it like a jelly roll. Fasten with skewers or twine. Place on a baking tin with a little water and bake in a hot oven. Baste every few minutes.

Cover with browned cracker crumbs and serve with catsup or Hollandaise sauce.

BOILED DINNER

1 slab of fresh beef, not too fat
salt
vegetables

Rub enough salt over the beef to corn it but not too much to make it salty. Let the meat stand for two or three days, judging time by size.

Wash the meat thoroughly in cold water and put it in a pot. Cover the meat with water and boil gently until quite tender.

Add vegetables as desired, judging quantity by strength of flavor desired.

Although simple to make, this dish requires judgment that will challenge even the most experienced cook. —Mrs. B.

DEVILED MEAT

cold rare beef, or under-cooked mutton, or cooked turkey or chicken
1 tablespoon butter
1 teaspoon vinegar
1 teaspoon Worcestershire sauce
½ teaspoon prepared mustard
pinch of cayenne

Make a sauce of the ingredients by mixing them together thoroughly. Make cuts in the meat and rub the sauce into the cuts.

Grill the meat in a pan that has been rubbed with butter. Serve hot.

In this recipe there's nary a word about ham. —Mrs. B.

BOILED HAM

12-lb. ham, uncured
cracker crumbs
black peppercorns
cloves

Put the ham on the fire in a large quantity of water and let it be an hour coming to a boil. Continue boiling slowly for three hours. Replenish evaporated water with boiling water so that the ham is always covered.

Take the ham out of the pot and remove the skin. Cover the ham with fine cracker crumbs and place it in a moderate oven to brown. Using peppercorns, create diamond patterns around the outside of the ham and center a clover in each diamond.

Wrap a ruffle of cut paper around the knuckle and serve with horseradish sauce.

HAM WITH MADEIRA

1 cured ham, not too salty
1 onion
1 carrot
1 dozen cloves
bay leaves

parsley
1 bottle Madeira
flour
butter

Place the ham in a kettle of water and heat it slowly. When scalding, remove the kettle from the fire and take out the ham. Scrape it clean and wash it well.

Return the ham to the kettle with sliced vegetables and two quarts of cold water. Bring to a boil and add cloves, a few bay leaves, a bunch of parsley and a bottle of Madeira wine. Simmer for three hours.

Skim off the fat and remove some of the liquid for gravy. It will have to be thickened with flour and butter.

Trim the skin off the ham, put a ruffle on the knuckle and serve.

Not only has this distinctive recipe been lost to time, but so has the delightful amber-colored dessert wine. —Mrs. B.

VIRGINIA HAM

1 uncured ham
1 teaspoon saltpeter
salt
hickory ashes
green hickory chips

Rub the saltpeter on the fleshy side of the ham, and salt overall but not too heavily. Let it stand for five weeks, six if weather is freezing. Brush off the salt, rub the ham with hickory ashes and let it stand for another week.

Hang the ham in a smoking shed fired with green hickory chips. Smoke for six weeks.

Pack the ham in hickory ashes until ready to use.

This recipe should give us an appreciation for what it takes to make a fine Virginia ham. We ought not take the name in vain as many meat packers do. —Mrs. B.

STEWED KIDNEYS

kidneys from veal, lamb or beef
flour
1 tablespoon butter
2 tablespoons tomato catsup
salt
black pepper

Soak the kidneys in vinegar and water for several hours. Rinse them well and parboil until tender.

Flour the kidneys and place them in a stewing pan. Add butter, catsup, salt and pepper and stew well.

The British still remember what a delicacy kidneys are. Regrettably, we seem to have forgotten. —Mrs. B.

POTATO CRUST

An excellent crust can be made from potatoes.

> **12 potatoes**
> **1 gill cream [½ *cup*]**
> **2 heaping tablespoons butter**
> **1 teaspoon salt**
> **flour**

Peel and boil the potatoes, and pass them through a sieve. Add cream, butter, salt and enough flour to form a paste.

PIG'S FEET

When cooked this way they are delicate and tender, and especially nice for frying, broiling or pickling.

Clean feet well and soak until very white. Wrap each foot in a piece of cloth and tie well with string. Boil for three to four hours and let stand in cloth until needed.

STEWED OX TAIL

2 ox tails
3 tablespoons butter
1 large onion
½ carrot
3 slices turnip
2 cloves
3 cups beef stock
salt
black pepper
flour

Skin and cut the ox tails into 3-inch pieces.

Cut the vegetables into small pieces and brown them in butter. Add a little flour and stir for three minutes. Put in the ox tails, add seasoning and stock, and simmer for three hours.

Cover with strained gravy and serve hot.

CURED PORK

200 lbs. fresh pork
sack of salt
2 ounces saltpeter

Sprinkle the pork with salt and place it in a vat for four or five days. Then remove the meat to a barrel and cover each layer with salt.

Dissolve enough salt in water to make a brine strong enough to float a potato. Add saltpeter to the brine and pour the brine over meat. Close the barrel tightly and let it stand undisturbed until needed.

BEEF STEW

2 lbs. stewing beef
1 tomato
onion
salt
black pepper
butter
flour

Cut the beef into small pieces and put it in a pot of cold water. Add the tomato, a little finely chopped onion and some salt and pepper. Cook slowly.

Thicken with butter and flour, and serve over toast

Note the unusual simplicity of this recipe—a far cry from what we usually think of as "old-fashioned" beef stew with its complex cooking instructions and ingredients. —Mrs. B.

VEAL OLIVES

fillet of veal ½-inch thick	**sweet marjoram**
salt pork	**cloves**
bread crumbs	**1 egg**
1 onion	**veal gravy (or light stock)**
salt	**butter**
black pepper	

Cut the veal into 3-inch squares. Chop up a little salt pork and combine it with bread crumbs, chopped onion, salt, pepper, marjoram, cloves and a well-beaten egg. Spoon the mixture onto the veal and fasten the four corners together with skewers.

Place the squares in a pan with enough gravy or stock to cover the bottom. Dredge [*coat heavily*] with flour and when well-browned on top, drop some butter on each.

Let stand for about twenty minutes, at which time they will be nice and tender. Serve with horseradish.

FRICANDEAU OF VEAL

4-lb. fillet of veal	**stock**
pork fat	**black pepper**
pork	**salt**
carrots	**parsley**
1 head of celery	**1 onion**

Lard the veal on top by making several cuts and inserting strips of pork fat.

Place a few thin slices of pork in a saucepan and cover them with some sliced carrots, a head of celery, an onion and some parsley.

Place the meat on top of the vegetables and season it with salt and pepper. Pour in enough boiling stock to cover the veal, put a lid on the saucepan and bake in moderate oven for two and one-half hours.

Be sure to baste several times.

This is larded veal, roasted and glazed in its own juices. —Mrs. B.

47

POULTRY

VIRGINIA FRIED CHICKEN

1 young chicken, dressed
½ lb. salt pork

black pepper
parsley

Cut up the chicken and soak the pieces in salty water. Dice and fry the salt pork until it's rendered into hot lard.

Dry the chicken, season it with pepper and dredge [*coat heavily*] every piece with flour.

Fry in hot lard until it attains a rich golden color. Serve with bunches of fried parsley.

BOILED CHICKEN

1 whole chicken, dressed

Wrap the chicken in a clean white cloth, put it in a pot, cover with water and boil slowly until done. Keep the pot covered so as little steam escapes as possible.

If young, the chicken will cook in one hour. If old, in two hours.

Make a gravy from the liquid by adding butter, flour, salt and pepper.

FRICASSEE OF CHICKEN

1 chicken, dressed
1 cup milk
1 heaping teaspoon flour
salt
back pepper
salt pork

Cut up the chicken and stew until tender in enough water to cover. Mix in the flour and milk and let it boil up once.

Season with salt and pepper.

A little salt pork may be added, cut in thin slices, a few minutes before serving.

GOOSE GIBLET PIE

2 sets of goose giblets	roux
1 carrot	1 glass sherry
1 onion	parsley
4 cloves	pie crust
parsley	cayenne
salt	2 shallots
black pepper	sweet basil
1 quart good broth	mushrooms
beef scallops	herbs

Clean and scald the giblets. Immerse in cold water, drain on a napkin and cut them into pieces about two inches long.

Put the cut giblets in a stewing pan. Add the carrot, an onion stuck with cloves, and a fagot [*bundle*] of parsley. Season with salt and pepper, moisten with broth and sherry and stew gently over a slow fire.

When done, remove the carrot, onion and parsley. Strain out the giblets and skim off the grease.

Thicken the broth with a little roux and boil it for fifteen minutes, stirring constantly with a wooden spoon. Reduce to about two cups and remove from the fire.

Cover the bottom of a dish with beef scallops and season with fine herbs, mushrooms, parsley, a little sweet basil and two shallots. Add some salt and cayenne.

Cover with half the sauce and fill the dish with giblets in neat order. Sprinkle with more fine herbs and pour the remainder of the sauce over everything.

Cover with pie crust, bake for one and one-quarter hours and send to the table.

ROAST GOOSE

1 goose	**flour**
bread crumbs	**salt pork**
apples	**sage**
onions	**black pepper**
salt	

Singe the goose and remove the pin feathers. Before it is cut and drawn, scrub thoroughly in soap suds to cleanse the pores and allow the oil to be more easily extracted. Draw, wash and rinse inside in clear water. Wipe dry.

Stuff the goose with equal parts of bread crumbs, chopped apples and boiled onions. Season with salt, pepper and sage. Sew up and truss the goose, set it on a rack in a pan and cover the breast with slices of salt pork.

Bake in an oven for ¾ hour. The pork fat will be drawn out quickly by the heat and flow over the goose. This will aid in drawing out the oil. After considerable oil is extracted, remove the pan from the oven and pour it off.

Remove the pork, dredge [*coat heavily*] the goose with flour and restore it to the oven. When the flour has browned, add a little hot water and baste often. Cook until brown and tender. Make gravy from drippings, garnish goose with watercress and serve with applesauce.

ROAST TURKEY

1 turkey, dressed	**butter**
bread crumbs	**flour**
salt pork	**black pepper**
sweet marjoram	**salt**

Stuff the turkey with a forcemeat made of bread crumbs, salt pork, marjoram, salt and pepper. Dredge [*coat heavily*] the turkey with flour. If it's not a very fat bird, put bits of butter about the breast and roast.

Turn the bird frequently until the flour begins to brown. Baste often with salt and liquid from the drip pan. When half done, dredge again with flour. If the breast is browning too quickly, place a piece of paper over it.

A turkey of ten pounds requires two and one-half hours of roasting with repeated basting.

Fifteen or twenty minutes before you wish to serve, drip a little melted butter over the turkey. Make a gravy from the giblets and serve with cranberry sauce.

TURKEY GIBLET GRAVY

turkey neck	**gizzard**
heart	**drippings**
liver	**flour**

Boil the neck and giblets in two cups of water. When tender, remove giblets and chop fine, rejecting the neck. Return chopped giblets to the liquid and add drippings from the roast pan. Skim off the fat, boil for a few minutes and thicken with a little browned flour.

ROAST TURKEY WITH OYSTER DRESSING

1 turkey, dressed	**sage**
salt	**1 tablespoon butter**
bread	**24 raw oysters**
black pepper	

After washing the turkey thoroughly, wipe it dry and rub it with a little salt. Make up a stuffing of diced bread, salt and pepper, sage, butter and oysters. Put the stuffing into the cavity and sew up or skewer the skin.

Bake for two and one-half hours, basting often.

ROAST TURKEY WITH CHESTNUTS

1 turkey, dressed
bread
1 dozen chestnuts
salt
black pepper
sage
sweet marjoram

Peel the chestnuts and boil them in their skins for five minutes in salt water. Peel off the skins and boil the chestnuts in fresh water until soft.

Prepare the turkey in the usual way for roasting. For dressing combine diced bread with chopped chestnuts and season with salt, pepper, sage and sweet marjoram.

Stuff the bird and roast it in the usual manner. Serve with currant jelly.

WILD GAME

ROAST CANVASBACK DUCK

1 canvasback duck, dressed
bread
port wine
butter
flour
lemon juice (or orange)

Truss the duck and insert a thick piece of bread that has been soaked in port wine. Place the duck over a quick fire and roast it for forty-five minutes to one hour.

Make a gravy by stewing the giblets slowly in as little water as possible. Thicken with butter rolled in flour.

Before sending to the table, squeeze over the duck the juice of a lemon or orange.

A "dressed" bird is not one with proper ruffles on its drumsticks. Rather it's one that has been cleaned and divested of all feathers, singed to remove all pinfeathers, properly eviscerated and otherwise made ready for cooking. "Dressed" game is skinned and similarly prepared. —Mrs. B.

GUINEA-FOWL

2 guinea-fowls per person, dressed   **bacon**
pork fat   **watercress**

Slice the skins of half the birds and lard them with strips of pork fat. Cover the remaining birds with strips of bacon.

Roast the birds over a brisk fire for about forty-five minutes. Glaze with wine sauce [page 80] and dish up with watercress. Pour a little gravy under the birds.

Serve with bread sauce in a boat.

PLOVER

1 plover per person, dressed
butter
salt
toast
black pepper

Clean and truss the birds. Season with salt and pepper and rub well with butter. Place them in a pan and roast in a quick oven.

Toast some bread and when the birds are nearly done, place a piece of toast under each bird. Baste well with butter and serve.

PARTRIDGE

partridges, dressed
boiled ham fat
butter
1 cup stock
1 tablespoon flour
2 tablespoons butter
lemon slices

Prepare as you would chicken but leave the feet on. Scald the feet, draw off their skins and skewer them up. Lard the breasts by slitting the skins and tucking in pieces of boiled ham fat.

Roast the birds for forty-five minutes over a moderate fire. Baste with butter before taking them up.

Serve with gravy made from stock, and flour and butter braided together. Garnish with slices of lemon.

Wild Game

PARTRIDGE PIE

5 partridges, dressed
salt
black pepper
flour
parsley
thyme
mushrooms
a few slices of ham
1 lb. veal, sliced
2 cups broth
pie crust

Split the birds in half. Rub them with salt and pepper and sprinkle on a little flour. Drop in some parsley, thyme and mushrooms.

In the bottom of a dish, layer the ham and veal slices. Add the partridges and pour the broth over them.

Place over the dish a good pie crust and bake for one hour.

PHEASANT

a brace of pheasants, dressed
2 tablespoons béchamel sauce, reduced
3 dozen mushrooms
4 black truffles
bread crumbs
white ragout

Roast the pheasants nicely. As soon as they come off the spit, cut the meat from their breasts by making an incision in the shape of a heart. Swiftly dice the meat with two dozen mushrooms, two truffles and mix in the reduced béchamel sauce.

Fill the breasts of the pheasants with the mixture and smooth it over with a knife blade. Cover with lightly fried bread crumbs.

Pour around the birds a white ragout made with the remaining mushrooms and truffles, and serve.

BROILED PIGEONS

Pigeons should not be kept for longer than six hours after being killed as they quickly lose their flavor.

> **pigeons, dressed**
> **butter**
> **salt**
> **slices of pork**
> **black pepper**

Split the pigeons down the back and broil as you would chickens. Season with salt, pepper and butter.

Broil some pork at the same time, place over each bird and serve.

STEWED PIGEONS

pigeons, dressed
salt pork
black pepper
bread
sour apples
salt
butter

See the note on pigeons in the previous recipe. —Mrs. B.

Cut strips of salt pork 1 inch long and one-half-inch wide. Roll the strips in pepper and place them in the cavity of each bird. Add a piece of bread about the same size and fill up the remaining space with bits of sour apple.

Place the pigeons breast down in a stewing pan and dredge [*coat heavily*] with flour. Add just enough water to cover, season with salt and pepper and stew over a moderate fire for one hour.

Serve in their own gravy.

POSSUM

1 nice fat possum, dressed   **sweet potatoes**
wood ashes

Bring a large kettle of water to a boil and shovel in some ashes. Dip the dressed possum into the hot water and scrape off all the hair and fur. Split the possum open, spread it flat and hang it in a tree for two to three nights.

Place the possum in a pan and completely bury it under slices of sweet potato. Cover and roast slowly over hot coals until tender. The flavor of possum will migrate into the potatoes, and the flavor of the potatoes will migrate into the possum.

PRAIRIE CHICKEN

prairie chickens, dressed   **butter**

Clean and wash the birds thoroughly in water with a little baking soda added. Rinse several times, wipe dry and stuff with a good dressing. Tie legs and wings down and stew. Cover closely and use plenty of butter.

When tender, remove chickens to a pan, brush with butter and brown. Serve with tart jelly.

QUAIL ON TOAST

quails, dressed
salt
black pepper
flour
butter
toast

Split the birds down the back and wipe them dry. Season with salt and pepper, and dredge [*coat heavily*] with flour. Pound the breasts flat and place the birds in a buttered pan with a little hot water. Roast covered until nearly done.

Finish by browning the birds in butter in a frying pan.

Place each quail on a well-buttered piece of toast, thicken the sauce with a little flour and pour it over them.

QUAIL PIE

quails, dressed
salt
black pepper
bread crumbs
(oyster dressing)
parsley
hard-boiled eggs
butter
flour
pie crust
lemon juice

Salt and pepper the clean quails. Stuff them with bread crumbs or oyster dressing and stew for a few minutes, well covered.

Overlay a dish with pie crust, add the birds and sprinkle them with minced parsley, chopped hard-boiled eggs and flakes of butter rolled in flour.

Add liquid from the stew pot, overlay pie crust and bake in a moderate oven for about one hour. A little lemon juice is a nice addition.

REED BIRDS

reed birds, dressed   **toast**
salt   **butter**
flour   **black pepper**

Tie the birds to a wooden skewer. Sprinkle with salt, dredge [*coat heavily*] with flour and roast over a quick fire for fifteen minutes. Serve on toast with butter and pepper.

In early times songbirds were a more important source of food than music. —Mrs. B.

SNOW BIRDS

snow birds, dressed   **salt**
oysters   **black pepper**
boiled pork   **pie crust**
butter

Stuff each bird with an oyster and place the birds in a dish. Add a little boiled pork and juice from the oysters. Season well with butter, salt and pepper.

Cover the dish with pie crust and bake in a moderate oven.

FRIED RABBIT

1 rabbit, dressed
eggs
cracker crumbs
salt
black pepper
butter

1 cup milk (or cream)
onion sauce
lemon slices
flour
lard

Boil the rabbit for a few minutes. When cold, cut it into joints. Dip the joints in beaten eggs, and roll them in cracker crumbs. Season with salt and pepper and fry them in butter and lard until brown.

Remove the pieces of rabbit to a serving dish. Thicken the gravy with a little flour, pour in the milk or cream and let it come to a boil.

Pour the gravy over the rabbit and serve hot with onion sauce. Garnish with lemon slices.

ROAST RABBIT

1 rabbit, dressed
bread crumbs
sausage meat
1 egg
salt
black pepper
1 onion
1 carrot

lemon slices
wine
flour
butter
bay leaf
peppercorns
cloves

Keep the cleaned and dressed rabbit in salted water for at least one hour. Stuff it with a mixture of bread crumbs, sausage meat and a well-beaten egg. Make sure to season the stuffing liberally with salt and pepper.

Sew up the rabbit, rub it with salt and pepper and place it in a roasting pan dressing side down. Add onion, cutup carrot, cloves, some peppercorns and a bay leaf. Drop bits of butter on the rabbit and sift flour over it. Add some hot water, cover closely and roast, basting often.

When done, place the rabbit on a platter, drip some wine over it and garnish with slices of lemon.

STEWED RABBIT

**1 rabbit, dressed
butter
1 tablespoon flour
onion
salt**

Cut the rabbit into pieces. Put a generous amount of butter into a stewing pan and brown the meat nicely.

Remove the meat and add two cups of boiling water.

Stir the flour into a paste with cold water and add it to the pan along with some grated onion. Salt to taste and let it boil up before putting the meat back in.

Stew slowly until tender, and serve hot.

BROILED SQUIRREL

1 squirrel, dressed   **black pepper**
butter   **lemon slices**
salt

Keep the dressed and cleaned squirrel in salted water for at least one hour, then wipe dry.

Broil over a hot fire, turning often. When done, brush with melted butter and season with salt and pepper. Garnish with lemon slices.

SQUIRREL PIE

a brace of squirrels   **flour**
salt pork   **butter**
seasoning   **pie crust**

Carefully skin and dress the squirrels. Cut into small pieces and place in a stewing pan. Add two slices of salt pork and enough water to stew the squirrels about half done.

Season and thicken the gravy with butter and flour. Transfer everything to a deep dish, cover with pie crust and bake in a moderate oven until done.

WILD TURKEY

bread crumbs	(cranberry sauce)
pork fat	currant jelly
salt	parsley
black pepper	lemon
milk	flour
1 egg	butter

Make a rich stuffing from bread crumbs, finely chopped pork fat, salt and pepper. Moisten with milk, beat in an egg and two tablespoons melted butter. Spoon stuffing into cavity.

Put the bird in a hot oven and baste with butter and water for the first hour. Then baste three or four times with juices. Lastly, baste five or six times with more melted butter. When almost done, dredge [*coat heavily*] the turkey with flour. When the flour turns brown, dredge the turkey with more butter.

Remove to a carving platter and garnish with sliced lemon and sprigs of parsley. Serve with currant jelly or cranberry sauce. For gravy, skim the drippings, add a little hot water and thicken with chopped giblets and browned flour. Boil up and pour into a boat.

Since nature did not endow wild turkeys with enough fat to ensure a juicy dish, our forebears generously made up for it. —Mrs. B.

TERRAPIN STEW

1 terrapin, dressed
salt
cayenne pepper
black pepper
a variety of spices
lemon
hard-boiled eggs
champagne

Parboil the meat, then mince it and season it well with all of the above. Stew until thoroughly done.

The result is very fine indeed.

Terrapin is the Algonquin word for turtle. As you can see from this recipe, it takes a lot of seasoning to turn one of these critters into a tasty stew. —Mrs. B.

Wild Game

VENISON STEAK

claret wine
currant jelly
venison steaks
butter
salt
black pepper

Heat a little claret wine, add a few spoonfuls of currant jelly and keep it warm.

Heat a grill over an open fire and grease it with butter. Put the steaks on the grill and broil rapidly, turning often to keep in the juices. When done, dip the steaks in a little melted butter, season with salt and pepper and ladle on the warm claret sauce.

HAUNCH OF VENISON

1 small haunch of venison	**stewed prunes**
4 carrots	**potato dumplings**
4 onions	**cherry sauce**
2 heads celery	**broth**
6 cloves	**1 bottle red wine**
parsley	**2 blades of mace**

Trim and remove the bone. Place the haunch in a braising pan with carrots, onions, celery, cloves, mace and a garnished fagot *[bundle]* of parsley. Moisten with a full bottle of wine and add enough broth to cover. Bring to a boil over brisk fire.

Remove haunch to a moderate oven and braise gently for five to six hours, basting frequently. When done, take up the haunch and put it in a deep baking dish with two cups of its own broth. Mask it with a thick coating of the following mixture:

1 lb. dried bread crumbs	**4 ounces sugar**
enough port wine to make a thick paste	**1 ounce cinnamon powder**

Smooth the mixture onto the haunch with a knife blade and place the haunch in a warm oven until crusty. Cover with cherry sauce and garnish with alternate layers of potato dumplings and prunes stewed in wine.

WINE SAUCE FOR ROAST GAME

3 cups fruit jelly
¾ lb. butter
3 tablespoons brown sugar
1 ½ tablespoons allspice
1 quart port wine

Combine ingredients and stew until thick.

May be used as accompaniment to any roasted meat, wild or tame.

This sauce will make any wild thing taste marvelous, absolutely marvelous. —Mrs. B.

FISH

BAKED FISH

any large fish, scaled and dressed	**black pepper**
bread crumbs	**parsley**
4 hard-boiled eggs	**1 small onion**
salt	

Dry fish carefully and stuff it with a dressing made from bread crumbs, hard-boiled eggs, parsley and onion, all finely chopped. Season with salt and pepper. Tie the fish with string to contain dressing and bake in a pan with a little water. Baste often to retain moisture.

Make a thick sauce from the following:

4 hard-boiled eggs	**2 tablespoons sugar**
½ cup vinegar	**a few white mustard seeds**
1 tablespoon butter	

Mash the eggs and combine with the remaining ingredients. Cook until stiff.

When the fish is done, place it on a platter and remove the string. Cover the fish with sauce and garnish with parsley and whites of two more hard-boiled eggs, neatly diced.

This recipe requires ten hard-boiled eggs so don't lose count! —Mrs. B.

BOILED FISH

any large fresh fish, scaled and dressed
1 tablespoon salt

Wash the fish and wrap it in cloth. Put the wrapped fish in pan of hot water and add salt. Adjust heat to maintain a slow movement of water for about thirty-five minutes.

Take out the fish, remove the cloth and serve [*the fish!*] with drawn butter

STEWED FISH

1 4-lb. fish, scaled and dressed   **2 tablespoons flour**
salt   **parsley**
black pepper   **thyme**
½ lb. butter   **3 hard-boiled eggs**

Season the fish with salt and pepper. Put it in a pot with two cups of water and let it stew. When half done, add salt, pepper, butter, flour, some parsley and a little thyme.

Serve as stew garnished with sliced hard-boiled eggs.

FISH BALLS

1 cup chopped cod
2 eggs, separated
2 cups mashed potatoes

1 tablespoon butter
lard

Beat the whites and yolks separately and combine with the other ingredients, making sure to mix well.

Form into balls and fry in hot lard.

FRIED PERCH

a mess of perch
salt

cornmeal
lard

Dress and skin the perch but leave the heads on. Salt the fish and roll them in cornmeal. Fry the perch in hot lard until golden brown.

Word to the wise: If you put fish in fat that's not very hot, it will break into pieces before it crisps.

FRIED SMELTS

a mess of smelts
milk
cracker dust
salt pork
lard
parsley

Clean nicely, handling as little as possible. Dip smelts in milk, then in cracker dust, then in beaten egg, then in dust again until abundantly coated.

Slice up a little salt pork and fry it in lard. Remove the pork and put in the smelts. Fry until golden brown.

Serve on a napkin and garnish with fried parsley.

SALT CODFISH

1 cup dried codfish
2 tablespoons butter
1 tablespoon flour

1 gill of cream [½ *cup*]
black pepper

Soak cod in tepid water for one hour.

Melt the butter and add the flour, stirring constantly. Transfer to a double boiler and add the codfish, the cream and a little pepper. Simmer for ten minutes, stirring constantly.

CODFISH BALLS

1 lb. dried codfish
1 dozen potatoes
salt
black pepper

½ cup milk
1 egg
lard

Soak the fish for one hour and then boil it to pieces. Pick what's left into shreds and let drain. Boil and mash the potatoes. Season with salt and pepper and combine with milk and egg. Add codfish shreds and form into balls. Fry in hot lard.

BAKED COD

1 codfish, scaled and dressed but not completely cut open
bread crumbs
fat pork
parsley
sweet marjoram
salt
black pepper
flour
tomato catsup

Prepare a forcemeat made from bread crumbs, fat pork, parsley, sweet marjoram, salt and pepper. Stuff the mixture into the fish and confine all openings with small skewers. Put four or five cuts on each side of the fish and dredge [*coat heavily*] with flour and salt.

Place the fish on a drip pan with enough water to cover the bottom. Bake until done. Baste with butter and tomato catsup.

For gravy, stir a little flour and butter into the drippings and serve hot.

VEGETABLES & SIDE DISHES

BOILED CABBAGE WITH BACON

1 head of cabbage
salt
1 lb. bacon
(red pepper)

Quarter a head of hard white cabbage and immerse it in cold salted water for two or three hours. Put the bacon in a large pot and boil it. Drain the cabbage and add it to the pot.

A little red pepper is discretionary but makes for a decided improvement.

SPICED CABBAGE

1 head of cabbage	**1 teaspoon peppercorns**
½ cup vinegar	**1 teaspoon cloves**
1 teaspoon sugar	**1 teaspoon salt**

Quarter the cabbage. Put it in a saucepan with vinegar, sugar, salt and spices. Cover and steam slowly until tender.

CABBAGE SALAD

½ head of cabbage
2 tablespoons flour
2 tablespoons butter
1 egg
1 cup vinegar
1 ½ teaspoons dry mustard
1 teaspoon black pepper
1 teaspoon salt
1 cup sweet cream

Finely chop the cabbage and set it aside.

Make a dressing by mixing the flour with the butter and adding egg, vinegar, mustard, pepper and salt. Cook until thick and allow to cool.

Add cream to the dressing and mix it into the chopped cabbage.

HOT SLAW

½ head of cabbage   **flour**
milk   **butter**
salt   **(egg)**
black pepper

Shave the cabbage fine. Put it in just enough water to cook and, when tender, add a little milk, salt and pepper. Rub some flour in butter and stir that in too. An egg may be used in place of flour.

WARM SLAW

1 hard red cabbage   **1 teaspoon salt**
butter   **cayenne**
2 gills water [1 cup]   **1 clove garlic**
3 gills vinegar [1½ cups]

Cut the cabbage by shaving down the head in very thin strips. In a saucepan melt a piece of butter the size of an egg. Add water, vinegar, salt, a little cayenne and some finely chopped garlic. Bring to a boil and pour it over the shaved cabbage. Cover closely for five or ten minutes. It is then ready for the table.

STEWED CELERY

1 head of celery	**salt**
cream	**black pepper**
butter	**nutmeg**
flour	

Clean the head nicely and take off all the outer leaves. Cut in small pieces and stew until tender.

Add cream, butter and very little flour. Season with salt, pepper and a hint of nutmeg.

ROAST CHESTNUTS

chestnuts	**salt**
butter	**cayenne**

Peel the chestnuts and scald them to remove the inner skin. Place them in a frying pan with a little butter and toss them around for a few minutes.

Add a little salt and a dainty sprinkle of cayenne.

93

CHEESE STRAWS

salt
½ ounce grated Parmesan cheese
¼ lb. puff pastry

Add a little salt to the cheese and sprinkle it over the pastry. Roll two or three times and cut the pastry into narrow strips about six inches long.

Bake in a slow oven and send to the table hot.

TOMATO CHOWCHOW

1 peck green tomatoes [8 *quarts*]
6 green peppers
1 onion
1 cup salt
vinegar
1 cup sugar
1 cup grated horseradish
1 tablespoon whole cloves
1 tablespoon cinnamon

Slice up the tomatoes, peppers and onion. Strew the vegetables with a cup of salt and let stand overnight.

Pour off any water and remove to a kettle. Pour in enough vinegar to cover and add sugar, horseradish, cloves and cinnamon.

Stew slowly until the peppers and onions are perfectly soft. The tomatoes will take care of themselves.

CORN PUDDING

3 eggs
2 cups fresh corn
1 quart milk

lump of butter
salt

Beat eggs and mix in corn, milk and butter. Put mixture into moderate oven and stir until thick. Add salt to taste and bake until brown. Cooking time is about one and one-half hours.

CORN OYSTERS

6 ears new corn
1 egg
1 tablespoon flour
1 tablespoon sweet cream

salt
black pepper
butter

Scrape the kernels off the cobs. Mix with lightly beaten egg, flour, cream and seasoning.

Make into oyster-size pats and fry in hot butter until light brown.

CUCUMBERS

Cucumbers should be harvested very early in the morning. After peeling, cucumbers should be kept in cold water until an hour before needed.

cucumbers	**black pepper**
onion	**1 cup vinegar**
salt	**1 lump of ice**

Slice as thin as possible and drop into fresh cold water until ready to serve. Drain off every drop of water and fill a dish with alternate layers of cucumber and thinly sliced onion. Season with salt and pepper, drench with vinegar and perch a lump of ice on top.

FRIED CUCUMBERS

cucumbers	**1 egg**
salt	**cracker dust**
black pepper	

Peel the cucumbers and slice them lengthwise. Let stand in cold water for about one hour. Wipe dry and season them with salt and pepper. Dip in a well-beaten egg, and then in cracker dust. Fry on both sides to a light brown.

EGGS AS A SIDE-DISH

hard-boiled eggs　　　　　　　　**black pepper**
bread crumbs　　　　　　　　　　**butter**
salt

Cut the eggs in half the long way. Remove the yolks and mix them with bread crumbs, salt, pepper and butter. Replace the enriched yolks. Bake briefly in an oven until the yolks (not the whites) are brown.

EGGS WITH FRIED POTATOES

cold boiled potatoes　　　　　　**1 egg per serving**
butter

Slice the cold boiled potatoes and fry them in butter until brown. Beat the eggs and stir them into the potatoes.

Be prepared to remove the pan from the fire almost immediately after the eggs have been added. When allowed to harden, eggs are not nearly as good.

BAKED EGGS

eggs
butter

salt
black pepper

Crack the eggs carefully into a dish so the yolks do not break. Turn them into a well-buttered graniteware pan and season with salt and pepper. Drop a small piece of butter on each egg and bake in a hot oven until the whites are set.

A lost art, more's the pity. —Mrs. B.

SNOW EGGS

1 quart milk

6 eggs

Separate the eggs and beat the whites to a stiff froth. Bring the milk to a boil and drop in the egg white one spoonful at a time. Turn each spoonful quickly, lift out with a skimmer and place on a sieve.

Beat the yolks and stir them into the milk. Allow one boil-up and remove to a glass dish. Arrange whites around the edges and serve cold.

99

HOMINY

Soak the hominy in water overnight. Wash well in the morning and boil until thoroughly done. Season and send to the table hot.

Hominy is corn that has been soaked in lye to remove the hull and germ. —Mrs. B.

HOMINY GRITS

1 teaspoon salt
5 cups water
1 cup hominy grits

Grits are hominy that has been coarsely ground. —Mrs. B.

Add the salt to the water, bring to a boil and add the grits. Cook for twenty to twenty-five minutes, stirring often.

OKRA

okra   **salt**
1 tablespoon butter   **black pepper**
½ cup sweet cream

Pick tender okra and boil in salted water until done. Drain well.

Add butter and cream, and season with salt and pepper. Serve hot.

PARSNIPS

Parsnips are better when left in the ground all winter.

parsnips   **cream**
butter   **(egg batter)**

When large, parsnips require boiling for at least one and one-half hours. When done, peel off the skin and split the parsnips in half. Serve with butter and cream.

Alternately, parsnips may be mashed, mixed with egg batter and seasoned.

BOILED ONIONS

onions
milk
butter
salt
black pepper

Take off the outer skins and soak the onions in cold water for two hours, longer if you like them mild.

Cook the onions in boiling water, strongly salted. When nearly done, drain off the water and simmer in milk until tender.

Add a good bit of butter and season with salt and pepper.

BAKED ONIONS

very large onions
bacon
bread crumbs
salt
black pepper
cream
butter

Skin the onions and parboil for one-half hour. Drain off the water and push out the hearts.

Chop the hearts fine along with a little bacon. Add some bread crumbs, season with salt and pepper and moisten with cream. Put it all back into the onions.

Place the stuffed onions on a drip pan with very little water. Cook until tender in a slow oven, basting often with melted butter.

PICCALILLI

This is chopped mixed pickles which may be cooked or preferably scalded.

1 peck green tomatoes [8 quarts]	**2 cups molasses**
2 cups salt	**2 ounces white mustard seed**
1 head of cabbage	**1 tablespoon allspice**
6 onions	**1 tablespoon cloves**
12 sweet peppers	**vinegar**

Slice tomatoes thinly, add salt and let stand in cold water for twenty-four hours.

Chop fine the cabbage, onions and sweet peppers. Cover with scalding vinegar and strain. Pack chopped vegetables into a jar, add vinegar, spices, molasses and mustard seed. Place the jar in pan of water and bring contents to a boil.

When cool, add the tomatoes.

PICKLES

cucumbers not more than 3 inches long
salt
cloves
spices

Pack the cucumbers in a crock with enough salt to make a strong brine. Water need not be added as cucumbers usually furnish enough moisture. Keep the cucumbers submerged by placing over them a weighted follower. They may remain in the crock until wanted for the table.

To preserve pickles, take them out of the brine and soak them in water until fresh. Pack them in jars and pour over them scalding vinegar that has been seasoned with cloves and spices.

If a fashionable green color is desired, first scald the pickles with boiling water in a brass kettle, and add a little alum to harden. Then pack them in jars with hot vinegar and spices.

QUICK PICKLES

small cucumbers
salt
1 gallon vinegar
1 cup molasses
1 tablespoon cloves
1 tablespoon cinnamon

Put the cucumbers in a porcelain kettle, cover with cold water, add some salt and heat gradually. After boiling five minutes, drain off the water and transfer the cucumbers to an earthen or stone dish.

To the vinegar, add molasses and spices and boil for five minutes. Pour the hot vinegar over the cucumbers and cover tightly.

Pickles are ready to use when cold.

INDIAN PICKLES

cucumbers
onions
1 or 2 garlic cloves
1 gallon vinegar

some grated ginger
handful of salt
6 ounces turmeric
½ lb. dry mustard

To the cold vinegar add mustard, turmeric, a handful of salt and a little grated ginger. Bring to boil and let cool.

Scald the vegetables with vinegar and place them in a jar with a small cloth bag containing:

¼ lb. ginger
1 ounce long red pepper pods
1 ounce black pepper
1 ounce cloves
½ ounce cayenne

From the character of the spices, we may assume these are East Indian pickles. —Mrs. B.

Fill the jar with the spiced vinegar that has been allowed to cool.

SWEET PICKLES

3 quarts sliced cucumbers
2 quarts vinegar
2 cups sugar
1 cinnamon stick
1 teaspoon pimento

Peel the cucumbers, remove the seeds and cut lengthwise into one-inch strips. Soak the strips in three cups of vinegar and four cups of water for twenty-four hours, stirring once or twice.

To one quart of vinegar add the sugar and the cinnamon stick. Tie the pimento in a bit of cloth and also add it. Bring the vinegar to a boil.

Add cucumber strips and cook until soft.

PIGS IN BLANKETS

2 cups oysters
½ lb. bacon

Drain and dry oysters. Wrap each oyster in a slice of bacon and secure with toothpicks. Cook in a hot pan until bacon is crisp. Serve on toast.

YORKSHIRE PUDDING

An accompaniment to roast beef.

4 eggs
9 tablespoons flour
2 cups milk
½ teaspoon salt

Beat the eggs and combine with flour, milk and salt. Place in the pan under the beef which should be roasting on a rack. Allow one-half hour to cook properly.

BOILED POTATOES

If you desire potatoes that are delicious and mealy, follow these directions faithfully.

Wash the potatoes well and let them stand in water for at least one and one-half hours. Never pare before boiling as they lose starch and become insipid.

Place the potatoes in a kettle with just enough cold water to cover. Potatoes produce a considerable quantity of fluid themselves and too much water makes them heavy. Add a little salt, cover and boil rapidly.

As soon as potatoes are done, instantly pour off the water and return the kettle to the heat long enough for the steam to evaporate.

The results are very satisfying.

Years ago, even simple potatoes were prepared with judicious and loving care. —Mrs. B.

KENTUCKY POTATOES

potatoes
salt pork
salt
black pepper
1 cup milk
1 cup boiling water

Pare the potatoes and slice them thin. Place the slices in a pan with bits of salt pork. Season with salt and pepper. Cover with milk and water and bake in a hot oven.

Remember that milk used to be quite creamy so if you try this recipe, you may want to forego the water. —Mrs. B.

POTATO CAKES

2 lbs. mashed potatoes
2 tablespoons butter
salt

2 lbs. flour
½ cup yeast
milk

Combine ingredients with a little salt and enough milk to make a batter. Set to rise and when light, bake in cakes the size of a muffin.

POTATO PUDDING

1 ounce suet
1 ounce cheese
1 ounce milk
12 ounces mashed potatoes

Chop the suet and cheese very fine and combine with milk and mashed potatoes. Add enough hot water to convert the mixture into a tolerably stiff mass.

Bake for a short time in an earthen dish either in front of the fire or in an oven.

POTATO DUMPLINGS

5 potatoes
1 ½ cups bread crumbs
1 tablespoon flour
1 tablespoon chopped parsley
1 tablespoon minced onion
1 ½ teaspoon salt
pinch of black pepper
2 eggs
1 tablespoon milk

Grate the potatoes and squeeze them dry in a napkin. Combine with remaining ingredients and shape into balls.

Coat lightly with flour and simmer in a suitable stew for fifteen minutes.

Vegetables & Side Dishes

QUIRLED POTATOES

potatoes
salt
black pepper
butter

Peel, boil, mash and season the potatoes. Press through a colander and into a serving dish.

Place in an oven long enough to brown.

SARATOGA POTATOES

potatoes
lard
salt

Peel and slice the potatoes as thinly as possible or use a slaw cutter. Drain and pat the slices dry.

Drop the potato slices into boiling lard a few at a time. Remove to a blotting pad and salt liberally.

114

SAUERKRAUT

No vinegar is used with this preparation.

cabbage
salt
caraway seeds
mace
allspice

Shred or shave the cabbage very fine. Pack it in a crock in six-inch layers. Between layers, strew a handful of salt, one-half cup caraway seeds and spices. Continue layering until the crock is full.

Put a thick strong cover over the cabbage and lay on a clean heavy weight. Cover with a cloth and let stand four weeks in winter and not quite two weeks in summer. At this time the cabbage will be in a state of fermentation.

Some people find sauerkraut to be quite delicious at this early stage. Traditionally, however, it is not taken out until all fermentation has ceased. This is usually indicated by a total lack of activity within the crock.

115

SALSIFY

salsify roots
butter
salt
black pepper
flour

Scrape and wash the roots and cut them in slices. Stew for twenty minutes in enough water to cover. Keep well covered or they will turn dark when exposed to air.

When done add butter, salt and pepper. Thicken with a little flour. Serve hot in a covered dish.

This root is also known as oyster plant. —Mrs. B.

BROILED TOMATOES

large tomatoes
salt
black pepper
butter

Place clean whole tomatoes on a gridiron over lively coals, stem side down. When brown, turn the tomatoes and let them cook until quite hot through and through. Remove to a hot dish and send quickly to the table with plenty of salt, pepper and melted butter on the side.

FRIED TOMATOES

tomatoes	**lard**
flour	**black pepper**
eggs	**salt**

Pour hot water over the tomatoes and peel. Cut into slices about one-half-inch thick.

Dip each slice into flour and then into beaten egg. Sprinkle with salt and pepper and fry in hot lard.

TURNIPS

Turnips are a very watery vegetable.

turnips	**salt**
cream	**black pepper**
butter	

To cook, place in hot water and boil thoroughly until well done, adding a little salt to the water. Drain and mash fine through a colander. Season with cream, butter, salt and pepper. Keep hot until you dish your dinner.

PORK AND TURNIPS

turnips
salt
black pepper
pork gravy

Boil turnips until done. Mash well and season with salt and pepper. Mix with pork gravy and place inside a hot oven for a few minutes. Serve hot.

RUSSIAN SALAD

6 salted herrings
6 anchovies, more or less
½ lb. smoked salmon
(roast turkey, chicken or veal)
pickles
capers
olives
mayonnaise
lettuce leaves
hard-boiled eggs

Soak herrings in water for twenty-four hours. Skin, remove bones and chop fine. Add some anchovies and smoked salmon, also chopped fine. (Cold roast turkey, chicken or veal may be added and is an improvement.)

To the above add a liberal amount of pickles, capers, olives and mayonnaise.

Line a salad bowl with lettuce leaves, fold in the salad and garnish with hard-boiled eggs.

HERRING SALAD

4 lbs. roasted veal
5 large beets
6 large potatoes
12 salted herrings
1 apple
1 onion
salt
black pepper
oil
vinegar
hard-boiled eggs

The day before, roast the veal and soak the herrings in cold water for twelve hours. Boil the potatoes and beets separately.

Fillet the herrings and cut them into small pieces. Do not hash! Cut up the veal, beets and potatoes the same way. Mix well. Add chopped apple and onion, and season with salt, pepper, oil and vinegar.

Garnish with hard-boiled eggs, beets and potatoes.

VEAL SALAD

1 veal cutlet
3 tablespoons vinegar
1 teaspoon sugar
¼ teaspoon salt
cayenne
prepared mustard
2 egg yolks
2 tablespoons cream
lettuce leaves

Boil the cutlet until tender in a little salt water. Then pick it to pieces.

Make a dressing of vinegar, sugar, salt, cayenne and prepared mustard. Put it on the fire and bring it to a boil. Pour gradually over the well-beaten yolks of two eggs. Cook until thick, stirring constantly. When cool, beat in the cream.

Mix half the dressing into the veal and keep it in a cool place. Just before serving, mix some shredded lettuce leaves into the veal. Fold into a dish lined with crisp lettuce leaves and cover with the remainder of the dressing.

SAUCES & DRESSINGS

ASPIC JELLY

For amber jelly, use beef stock. For white, use chicken or veal.

3 cups clear stock
½ box gelatine
½ cup cold water
pinch or two of salt
1 stalk of celery
3 cloves
2 slices of onion
1 dozen peppercorns
1 egg white

Soak the gelatine in the water for one and one-half hours. Add salt, celery, cloves, onion and peppercorns.

Beat the egg white with a spoonful of the cold stock and add it to the gelatine.

Put the mixture over the fire. When it begins to boil, move to a gentler heat where it can simmer slightly for twenty-five minutes.

Strain through a cloth, pour into a mold and set in a cold place to stiffen.

BARBECUE SAUCE

½ lb. butter
1 tablespoon dry mustard
½ teaspoon red pepper
½ teaspoon black pepper
salt
strong vinegar

Over a gentle fire, melt the butter and mix in the mustard and peppers. Add some salt and vinegar to taste. If the sauce does not have enough bite, add another pinch or two of red pepper.

When the meat has become heated through, begin to baste with the sauce. Baste often until the meat is sufficiently cooked.

BREAD SAUCE

Especially nice when served with roast turkey, fowl or game.

> **1 onion**
> **2 cups milk**
> **¾ lb. dry bread crumbs**
> **1 ounce butter**
> **mace**
> **salt**
> **cayenne**

Cut up the onion and boil tender in the milk. Strain the milk over the bread crumbs. Cover and let stand long enough to soak up the milk, then beat thoroughly. Add butter along with mace, salt and cayenne to taste. Boil up and serve.

If the sauce is too thick, thin it with cream but only after the sauce is made.

BUTTER SAUCE

2 tablespoons flour
½ cup butter
1 tablespoon lemon juice
cayenne

Work the flour into the butter until light. Place on the fire and gradually add one cup of boiling water. Stir constantly until it comes to a boil. Take from the fire immediately and serve with lemon juice and a pinch of cayenne.

DRAWN BUTTER SAUCE

½ cup butter
1 light tablespoon flour
salt

In a saucepan, mix the flour into the butter with two or three tablespoons of boiling water.

Shake the saucepan continually over the fire, allowing the contents to simmer but not boil. When the sauce is acceptably thick, it is ready to use.

CABBAGE DRESSING

2 eggs
butter the size of an egg
1½ teaspoons mustard
2 teaspoons flour

vinegar
salt
black pepper

Beat the eggs lightly. Without cooking, mix in the remaining ingredients over a tolerable fire.

When hot, pour the dressing over cooked cabbage and serve.

CELERY DRESSING

2 eggs
butter
1 teaspoon prepared mustard

½ cup vinegar
¼ teaspoon salt
1 cup sweet cream

Beat the eggs lightly and mix in the remaining ingredients. Put over fire and boil until you attain the proper consistency.

Allow to cool before serving over cooked chopped celery.

CATSUP

Catsup is a semi-liquid condiment that can be made from tomatoes, green walnuts, mushrooms or any similar ingredient that will impart a pleasant flavor.

tomatoes
salt
ground mustard
black pepper
allspice
cloves
cayenne
cider or wine vinegar

Scald the tomatoes and press through a sieve fine enough to retain seeds and skins.

To each gallon thus prepared, when cold, add four tablespoons of salt, three of ground mustard, two of black pepper, one of allspice, half as much of cloves, and half again as much cayenne pepper. Stir in two cups of your strongest cider or wine vinegar.

Simmer the whole together for four hours. Bottle and cork tight.

CELERY SAUCE

½ cup butter
1 tablespoon flour
1 cup milk
4 heads of celery
mace
salt
black pepper

Make a nice sauce out of the butter, flour, milk and a dash of salt.

Boil the celery in salted water until tender. Chop very fine and add to the butter sauce. Add mace, and season with salt and pepper.

CHILI SAUCE

A good substitute for tomato catsup and actually quite superior overall.

9 ripe tomatoes, peeled
4 onions
4 red peppers
4 cups vinegar
3 tablespoons sugar
2 tablespoons salt
2 teaspoons cinnamon
2 teaspoons allspice
2 teaspoons cloves
2 teaspoons ginger
2 teaspoons nutmeg

Combine the ingredients and boil for one hour.

COLD MEAT SAUCE

This will add zest to any cold meat dish.

3 egg yolks
2 ounces fruit jelly
1 tablespoon flour
1 tablespoon dry mustard
2 ounces vinegar
1 tablespoon butter
1 pickle

Beat the yolks and mix in some chopped jelly. Season with flour and mustard softened with a drop of vinegar.

Put the whole in a sauce pan with butter and vinegar and boil until thick, taking care to stir constantly.

When the sauce is cold, chop up some pickle and mix it in.

EGG SAUCE

Especially nice with fish when served hot.

5 or 6 hard-boiled eggs
1 cup melted butter or white sauce
cream

Chop up the eggs and mix in the butter or white sauce with a little cream.

GHERKIN SAUCE

6 green gherkins   **white sauce**
tarragon vinegar   **veal**
black pepper

Slice the gherkins thinly and place them in a small stewing pan with a little tarragon vinegar and some pepper. Simmer briskly for a few minutes, then add a small quantity of white sauce and a bit of veal.

Stir sauce until it boils, then set aside until it clears. Skim and pour into a dish for use.

HORSERADISH SAUCE

4 tablespoons grated horseradish
1 teaspoon salt
1 teaspoon sugar
½ teaspoon black pepper
2 teaspoons prepared mustard
2 teaspoons vinegar
3 or 4 tablespoons cream

To the grated horseradish add the remaining ingredients and stir well. Serve cold.

With roast beef, serve hot by heating the sauce in a jar placed in boiling water. Do not allow the sauce to boil or it will curdle.

The biggest challenge in this recipe lies not in finding the horseradish root, but in grating it without weeping a bucket. —Mrs. B.

LEMON SAUCE

Nice with stewed poultry.

> **soup stock**
> **lemon**
> **sugar**
> **nutmeg**
> **parsley**
> **nasturtiums**
> **black pepper**
> **flour**
> **(egg yolks)**

Boil some soup stock with a few slices of lemon, a very little sugar and a wisp of grated nutmeg. Add to this some chopped parsley, a few nasturtiums and a very small taste of pepper.

The sauce may be thickened with a little flour or egg yolks.

SIMPLE MAYONNAISE

Easily made and very nice.

1 egg yolk
1 teaspoon dry mustard
¼ teaspoon white pepper
cayenne
1 lemon
3 gills salad oil [*1½ cups*]
4 tablespoons strong vinegar

Using a wooden spoon, mix until creamy the egg yolk, mustard, pepper and a pinch of cayenne with the juice of half a lemon. Add the salad oil drop by drop, stirring constantly.

If the dressing thickens too fast, add a little juice from the other half of the lemon. Finally, add the vinegar a little at a time.

MINT SAUCE

To be made a few hours before serving.

2 teaspoons chopped mint   **1 cup vinegar**
1 teaspoon sugar

Use only fresh young leaves. Pick the leaves off the stalk and mince them very fine. Pour over them the sugar and vinegar. Stir well and serve with roast lamb, veal or pork.

MUSHROOM SAUCE

2 ounces butter   **salt**
1 teaspoon flour   **black pepper**
6 ounces milk   **paprika**
1 cup mushrooms

Mix the butter and flour together in a saucepan until smooth. Add the milk and heat over a brisk fire, making sure to stir in one direction. Simmer for a minute or two.

Add the mushrooms and let simmer for about ten minutes. Season with salt and pepper, and a dash of paprika for color.

MUSTARD

Mustard should always be mixed with water that has been boiled and allowed to cool. Make only enough to fill the mustard pot half way since mustard is better when freshly made.

ground mustard
salt
water

Put the mustard in a cup with a pinch of salt and gradually mix in enough water to allow it to drop from a spoon without being watery.

Stir well and rub away all lumps with the back of a spoon. Transfer to a suitable mustard pot for serving.

ONION SAUCE

Many people are fond of a sauce of onions, which are healthy and to most palates agree-able. Were it not for the unpleasant odor they give the breath, onions would be universally used both as food and flavoring.

4 large onions
1 cup milk
butter

salt
black pepper

Peel the onions and boil them until tender. Drain and chop very fine. Add the milk, a small lump of butter, and salt and pepper to taste. Heat (do not boil!) and serve.

PARSLEY SAUCE

1 bunch of parsley
salt

butter
cayenne

After washing the parsley, boil for five minutes in salted water. Drain well, cut the leaves from the stalks and chop them fine. Stir the leaves into a judicious amount of melted butter and add a pinch of cayenne.

RASPBERRY VINEGAR

This same formula may be used with other small fruits.

The entire process should be carried out in a glazed kettle or earthen vessel.

> **6 lbs. ripe raspberries**
> **2 quarts vinegar**
> **8 lbs. sugar**

To the clean and washed raspberries add your best vinegar and let stand for four days. Stir frequently but take care not to mash the fruit so as to bruise the seeds and liberate their bitterness.

Filter the vinegar through a clean cloth and stir in the sugar. Put it into a glazed jar or pan, which place in boiling water until the juice boils thick and syrupy.

Let it become cold, then bottle it.

TOMATO SAUCE

ripe tomatoes
garlic
(shallots)
ginger
black pepper
salt
lemons

Put any quantity of ripe tomatoes in a covered earthen jar and place in a hot oven. When soft, rub the tomatoes through a fine sieve to keep out the seeds and skins.

To every quart of juice add one clove of garlic (or two bruised shallots), one-quarter ounce of ginger, the same of black pepper, and one tablespoon of salt. The juice of two lemons may or may not be added, at the discretion of the cook. Boil for about twenty minutes.

While hot, put the sauce in a bottle, cork it down and wax at once.

WHITE SAUCE

2 tablespoons butter
2 tablespoons flour
2 cups milk
½ teaspoon salt
white pepper

Melt the butter and add the flour. Cook until smooth. Remove to a double boiler and add the milk slowly. Cook until creamy, stirring all the while. Season with salt and pepper.

WINE SAUCE FOR MEAT

¾ lb. butter
3 cups fruit jelly
¾ cup brown sugar
1 tablespoon allspice
1 quart port wine

To the melted butter add the remaining ingredients and stew until thick.

WORCESTERSHIRE SAUCE

Worcestershire sauce is generally adulterated. If made according to this formula it will be good and pure. Asafetida is an odorous condiment that imparts a bitter flavor. In India and Persia it is thought to stimulate the brain. It can also be used as a remedy for colic or as a palliative for bronchitis and the whooping cough.

20 lbs. hog livers	½ lb. cloves
10 gallons water	1 lb. powdered coriander
¼ lb. asafetida	1 lb. powdered allspice
1 gallon brandy	½ lb. mace
15 gallons white wine vinegar	½ lb. cinnamon
10 gallons walnut catsup	5 gallons Madeira wine
10 gallons mushroom catsup	4 gallons Canton soy sauce
2 lbs. powdered capsicum [*red pepper*]	twenty-five lbs. salt

Boil the hog livers in the specified amount of water for twelve hours, renewing the water from time to time. Dissolve the asafetida in the specified amount of brandy and mix it with the remaining ingredients and spices. Chop up the cooked livers, mix with water and work through a sieve. Stir the livers into the sauce and bottle for later use.

If you have the courage and the determination to try this recipe, consider dividing the ingredients by at least ten—maybe even one hundred! —Mrs. B.

CAKES, PIES & DESSERTS

BACHELOR'S PUDDING

A splendid dish.

> **3 eggs**
> **1 cup milk**
> **½ cup sugar**
> **1 soda cracker**
> **1 orange**

Beat the white of one of the eggs until firm enough to cut with a knife.

Beat well the remaining yolk with the other two eggs and mix in the milk and sugar. Break the cracker into six pieces, adorn with a slice of peeled orange and float in the dish.

Bake in a very hot oven until nearly done. Put a spoonful of the egg-white on each cracker, return to the oven and bake for five more minutes.

BROWN BETTY

1 cup bread crumbs
2 cups tart apples, chopped
½ cup sugar
1 teaspoon cinnamon
2 teaspoons butter, cut into small pieces
cream

Butter a deep dish and start with a layer of chopped apples at the bottom. Sprinkle with sugar, a few bits of butter and cinnamon. Cover with bread crumbs and add more chopped apple. Proceed in this fashion until the dish is full, ending with a layer of crumbs on top.

Cover closely and steam for ¾ hour in a moderate oven. Uncover and brown quickly.

Serve in the dish in which it has been baked. Eat warm with sugar and cream.

CAKE

2½ lbs. flour
1¼ lbs. pulverized white sugar
10 ounces soft butter
5 eggs, well beaten
⅛ ounce carbonate of ammonia [*baking powder*]
2 cups milk

Work the ingredients into a nice dough. Roll it out, cut it into cakes and bake.

While yet hot, dredge [*coat heavily*] with coarse sugar.

CAKE FROSTING

A glazed shallow earthen dish should be used.

Use ¼ lb. sugar for each egg white. Sprinkle the egg whites with part of the sugar and beat, adding sugar from time to time.

Lemon juice and tartaric acid whiten the frosting. If used, more sugar will be required. Flavoring such as vanilla should be added last.

Dredge [*coat heavily*] the cake with flour after it is baked, then wipe it carefully. This will enable the frosting to be spread more kindly.

Apply the frosting in large spoonfuls, beginning in the center. Spread it with a thin-bladed knife or spatula dipped from time to time in cold water.

CHRISTMAS CAKE

2 eggs
½ cup butter
1 cup molasses

1 cup raisins
2 cups flour
various spices

Mix and bake in a rather brisk oven.

COFFEE CAKE

This cake is much nicer for dipping in coffee if it is not cut until several days old.

2 cups flour
½ cup brown sugar
½ cup molasses
½ cup strong coffee, lukewarm
1 egg

1 cup butter
1 teaspoon baking soda
1 lb. raisins
spices

Combine the ingredients with plenty of spices and bake until done.

COOKIES

1 cup sugar
½ cup butter
½ teaspoon saleratus [*baking soda*]
½ cup sour cream
2 eggs
nutmeg
sugar
flour

Blend the sugar and butter. Add the saleratus to the sour cream and mix with well-beaten eggs with enough flour to roll out soft. Season with nutmeg.

Roll thin and sprinkle with sugar. Roll lightly and only once. Cut into desired shapes and bake in a quick oven.

DELICATE CAKE

This recipe will make a two-quart basin loaf.

If the proportions are followed unerringly, a beautiful cake will be the result.

> **1½ cups sugar**
> **½ cup soft butter**
> **½ cup milk**
> **½ teaspoon baking soda**
> **2 cups flour**
> **1 teaspoon cream of tartar**
> **salt**
> **vanilla**
> **4 egg whites**

Rub the sugar and butter into a cream. Add the milk, in which dissolve the baking soda. Then add the flour, in which rub the cream of tartar. Add a little salt and flavor with vanilla.

Beat the egg whites into a stiff froth and add last.

Bake slowly for one hour in a moderate oven.

DROP CAKES

1 lb. flour
½ lb. sugar
½ lb. butter
3 eggs
½ lb. currants
¼ lb. citron
1 teaspoon mace or cinnamon

Beat the butter and some of the flour to a cream. Separate the eggs and add the beaten yolks and some flour and sugar. Finally add the beaten whites and the remainder of the flour and sugar.

Stir in the currants, citron and mace or cinnamon. Drop with a spoon upon flat tins and sift sugar over them. Bake.

DROP JOHNNIES

2 eggs
1 cup sugar
1 cup cream
3 cups buttermilk
1 heaping teaspoon saleratus [*baking soda*]
salt
spices
flour
hot lard

Beat the eggs and mix in the sugar, cream, buttermilk and saleratus. Salt and spice to taste.

Thicken with flour to a stiff batter and drop in hot lard a spoonful at a time. Fry just as you would fried cakes.

EVE'S PUDDING

½ lb. apples
½ lb. bread crumbs
2 cups milk
½ lb. currants
6 ounces sugar
2 eggs
1 lemon

Chop the apples small. Add the bread crumbs, currants, sugar and the grated rind of the lemon. Beat the eggs well and add them.

Boil for three hours in a buttered mold and serve with sweet sauce.

FRIED CAKES

4 cups white sugar
4 cups buttermilk
1 cup butter
2 eggs
2 teaspoons baking soda
cinnamon to taste

Combine the ingredients and stir until quite hard. Roll out to a thickness of one-half-inch and cut into rings.

They will fry much nicer than when twisted.

HOMELY PIE

This recipe yields two pies.

1 cup molasses
1 cup vinegar
1 cup water
1 teaspoon extract of lemon
butter the size of an egg
cornstarch

Combine all the ingredients except the cornstarch which should be used for thickening after the mixture is brought to a boil.

Pour into crust-lined tins but do not put on a top crust as there is danger of its foaming over. Instead, strips of pastry may be laid across the top.

Bake until the crust is done.

LADY FINGERS

4 eggs
¼ lb. sugar
¼ lb. flour
butter

Beat the yolks with the sugar until smooth and light. Whisk the whites and add them. Sift in the flour.

Make into a smooth paste and lay on buttered paper in the size and shape the cakes are desired.

Bake quickly. While still hot, press two of the cakes into one on the flat side.

LEMON PIE WITHOUT LEMON

Many prefer this dish to pie made with real lemons.

½ teaspoon tartaric acid
½ cup cold water
1 teaspoon sugar
1 egg
½ teaspoon extract of lemon
1 soda cracker

Dissolve the tartaric acid in the water. Stir the egg yolk and sugar together and mix them into the water. Then add the lemon extract and crumble in the cracker.

Bake in a crust and cover with the beaten white of an egg. Return to the oven just long enough to brown.

MINCEMEAT FOR PIES

1½ ounces cinnamon
¾ ounce cloves
3 lbs. beef
9 quarts green apples, quartered
3 lbs. raisins
9 cups hard cider (or 5 cups vinegar and 4 cups water)
6 lbs. sugar (or 12 cups pressed full and rounded)
1½ cups suet, cut fine (or butter)

Grind the cinnamon and cloves together. Mix with the remaining ingredients in a kettle and simmer until heated through.

Pack into jars for later use.

MOONSHINE

1 cup tart fruit jelly
8 egg whites
sugar
6 ounces sweet cream

Before appropriated by illegal distillers, moonshine used to mean a little nothing. —Mrs. B

Beat jelly until easy to work. Beat whites of six eggs to a stiff froth and add six tablespoons sugar. Stir in jelly and beat until stiff enough to stand high on a flat dish.

Make a sauce by beating whites of two eggs to a stiff froth. Add sugar to taste and some lemon or vanilla. Beat in the cream and continue beating until the whole mixture is stiff.

Serve moonshine in pretty dishes and pile sauce on top.

PORK CAKE

      1 lb. fat pork
      2 cups boiling water
      1 lb. raisins, stoned and chopped
      1 cup molasses
      2 cups sugar
      8 cups flour
      1 tablespoon ground cloves
      1 tablespoon cinnamon
      1 tablespoon saleratus [*baking soda*]
      1 egg

Chop the pork very fine and cover with boiling water. Mix in the raisins, molasses, sugar, flour, spices, saleratus and egg—the white to be added last.

Pour the batter into a baking pan and place into a moderate oven until done.

POUND CAKE

1 lb. sugar
1 lb. butter
1 lb. flour
10 eggs
2 ounces brandy or cognac
½ nutmeg, ground fine
1 teaspoon vanilla

Beat the sugar and butter to a cream. Whisk the eggs to a froth and beat all the ingredients together until perfectly light.

Bake in a moderately heated oven for one hour. Turn the cake out of the tin, invert the tin, and set the cake on it to cool.

Apply frosting when cold.

POTATO PIE

1 cup mashed potatoes
1 cup sugar
½ cup butter

½ cup sweet cream
2 eggs
nutmeg

Combine the ingredients and flavor to taste with nutmeg. Bake in an under crust.

PEACH PIE

peaches
sugar
cream

Line a dish with a good pie crust.

Place in it a single layer of peach halves. Sprinkle sugar over them and pour on enough cream to fill the dish.

Bake without an upper crust.

QUAKER PUDDING

bread
butter
raisins
5 eggs
1 quart milk
salt
spices

Boil the raisins in very little water to make them tender.

Butter slices of bread and place in a pudding dish. Spoon raisins and their water onto the bread and cover with a layer of buttered bread. Alternate until dish is nearly full.

Beat eggs well and add milk. Salt and spice to taste. Pour over the bread and raisins and bake for one-half hour.

RAISIN PIE

Makes three pies.

1 lb. raisins
1 quart water
1 lemon
1 cup sugar
3 tablespoons flour
1 egg

Boil the raisins in a quart of water for one hour. Keep adding water so the quantity remains constant.

Grate the rind of the lemon into the sugar and mix well with the flour and egg. Add the raisins, stirring all the while.

Pour the mixture into a crust-lined tin and bake with a top crust.

RHUBARB PIE

rhubarb
flour
butter
2 ounces sugar

Prepare the stalks by peeling off the thin reddish skin. Cut into one-half-inch pieces and spread evenly in crust-lined tins.

Sift on a little flour, to which add bits of butter and the sugar.

If a very sharp, sour taste is not relished, a pinch of baking soda may be used to advantage with less sugar as it goes far toward neutralizing the acid.

SODA CAKES

1 teaspoon cream of tartar
1 teaspoon baking soda
1 tablespoon lard
1 tablespoon butter
4 cups flour
salt
buttermilk

Dissolve the cream of tartar salts in hot water.

Rub the lard and butter into the flour and add to it the cream of tartar, the baking soda and a little salt. Mix soft with some buttermilk and cut with a tin into round cakes.

Bake in a quick oven.

SHORTCAKE

2 cups flour
butter the size of an egg
2 teaspoons cream of tartar

1 teaspoon saleratus [*baking soda*]
1 cup cold water

Rub well into the flour the butter, cream of tartar and saleratus. Add water and make a stiff batter. Add flour as needed. Bake on tin for tea.

STRAWBERRY SHORTCAKE

dough [as in FANCY STRAWBERRY SHORTCAKE]
strawberries
sugar
cream

Make a nice dough and roll it out in thin cakes about the size of a breakfast plate. Put the first cake in the bottom of a baking dish, cover with a layer of strawberries and sprinkle lightly with sugar.

Add another cake of dough and another layer of strawberries and sugar. Top with a layer of dough. Serve with sweet cream.

FANCY STRAWBERRY SHORTCAKE

salt	**butter**
1 cup sugar	**flour**
6 cups ripe strawberries	**1 cup cream**
1 teaspoon baking soda	

Stir the sugar into the berries and let stand covered whilst you prepare the dough.

Beat a little salt and the baking soda into the cream. Before it stops foaming stir in enough flour to enable you to roll it out. Be sure not to get it very stiff.

Roll the dough into three circles, spread butter on top of each and place one on top of the other. Bake until well done.

Pull the layers apart. Butter one and cover it with strawberries. Butter the second and lay it crust downwards on top of the first. Add another layer of strawberries and cover with the third crust.

Place in the oven for a few minutes, remove and cover the top crust with large strawberries. Serve hot with cream.

Pounded ice is an excellent topping. Wrap the ice in a clean coarse towel and pound fine with a potato masher.

SNOW CUSTARD

8 eggs
1 quart milk
1½ cups sugar
1 teaspoon lemon juice

Add the eggs to the milk, leaving out the whites of four. Stir into this one-half cup of sugar. Put a shallow pan of hot water in the oven and set in it the dish of custard. Bake until thick, then set aside to cool.

Beat the four whites solid and stir in one cup of sugar and the lemon juice.

When the custard is cold, lay the whites over the top in heaps but do not let them touch.

SPONGE CAKE

This will make three good-sized loaves.

1 lb. sugar
10 eggs
2 lemons
¾ lb. flour

Separate the eggs and beat the sugar into the yolks. Grate into this the yellow rind of both lemons and add the juice of one.

Beat the egg whites very light and stir them into the mixture. Then stir in the flour but without beating.

Divide the batter equally into three greased or buttered pans. Care must be taken not to put them in too hot an oven.

SOUR CREAM PIE

2 eggs
1 cup sugar
1 cup sour cream
1 teaspoon vanilla

Beat the eggs well and mix in the sugar and sour cream. Stir thoroughly and add the vanilla. Bake with two crusts.

SYLLABUB

½ lb. fine white sugar
1 quart sweet cream
12 ounces Madeira or sherry

Mix the sugar into the cream and set aside for a few minutes. Add wine, whip to a stiff froth with an egg beater and serve in glasses.

STEAMED PUDDING

3 eggs
1 cup suet, chopped very fine
1 cup molasses
1 cup sour milk
1 teaspoon cinnamon
½ teaspoon cloves
1 teaspoon baking soda
1 cup raisins, chopped
4 cups flour
sugar
butter or milk

Sour milk is rarely found in the kitchen these days. A reasonable substitute may be made by adding one-half teaspoon vinegar to a cup of milk. —Mrs. B.

Beat the eggs and mix in the suet, molasses, sour milk, spices, soda, raisins and flour.

Put the mixture in a pudding dish and place the dish on a rack in a kettle of boiling water. Cover and steam for two hours.

Serve with sugar and butter or sugar and milk.

SUET PUDDING

½ cup suet, chopped very fine
½ cup sour milk
1 teaspoon saleratus [*baking soda*]
flour
½ cup raisins
½ cup currants
1 teaspoon allspice
3 eggs

Mix the suet into the milk and add saleratus. Stir in a little flour to make it stiff. Combine with fruit, spices and beaten eggs.

Boil for three hours.

TEA CAKE

1 egg
milk
1 cup sugar
½ cup butter
nutmeg
1 teaspoon saleratus [*baking soda*]
1 teaspoon cream of tartar
flour

Break the egg into a teacup [*four ounces*]. Fill the cup with milk and pour it into a mixing bowl. Add the sugar, butter, nutmeg, saleratus and cream of tarter. Stir in some flour until it's the consistency of common sponge cake.

Bake in a moderate oven until done.

WIDOW'S CAKE

A palatable cake to be eaten at tea as bread or rusks.

> **2 cups flour**
> **1 cup cornmeal**
> **1 teaspoon baking soda**
> **1 cup molasses**
> **2 eggs**
> **salt**
> **milk**

Mix the ingredients with just enough warm milk to make a batter.

Bake in a quick oven until done.

SWEETS & SUCH

BISQUE

1 gallon boiled custard
3½ lbs. macaroon almonds

Make a very rich custard and add the almonds before removing it from the fire. When cold, freeze.

CANDIED FRUIT

preserved fruit
1 lb. sugar
2 ounces water

After peaches, plums, citrons or quinces have been preserved, take the fruit out of the syrup and drain it well.

Mix the sugar and water together and place over a moderate fire. When boiling hot, add fruit and stir until the sugar is candied about it. Then take it up on a sieve and dry it in a warm oven or before a fire.

MOLASSES CANDY

2 tablespoons sugar
1 cup molasses

½ teaspoon baking soda
butter

Mix the sugar into the molasses and boil rapidly for twenty minutes. Stir constantly to keep from burning. Try if sufficiently brittle by dropping into cold water.

When done, rub the baking soda smooth and stir dry into the boiling candy. Mix thoroughly and pour into a buttered pan. Do not pull.

MOLASSES PULL CANDY

2 cups molasses
a lump of butter the size of a hickory nut

1 tablespoon vinegar
1 cup sugar

Combine the ingredients and boil briskly for twenty minutes, stirring all the while. When cool, pull until white.

SUGAR CANDY

6 cups sugar
1 cup vinegar
1 cup water
1 tablespoon butter
1 teaspoon baking soda
flavoring

Combine the sugar, vinegar, water and butter. Add the baking soda after it has been dissolved in a little hot water. Boil without stirring.

When the candy becomes hard but not brittle (test by dropping in cold water), flavor with lemon, wintergreen or peppermint and turn out on buttered plates to cool.

It is nice pulled or left on the plate and cut in squares.

CHOCOLATE CARAMELS

1 cup molasses
1 cup brown sugar
1 cup milk
½ cup grated chocolate
a lump of butter the size of an egg

Combine the ingredients and boil for one-half hour.

FUDGE

2 squares bitter chocolate
2 cups sugar
½ cup milk
1 teaspoon vanilla
a lump of butter the size of an English walnut

Mix together the ingredients and boil for nine minutes. Remove from heat and beat for five minutes.

Spread on a buttered pan and cut into squares.

APPLE CREAM

6 large apples
sugar

6 egg whites
cream

Peel and core the apples. Boil them in a small quantity of water until they can be pressed through a sieve. Sweeten to taste.

Beat the egg whites and mix with the strained apples. Serve in a glass dish with cream poured over them.

CHOCOLATE CREAM

1 quart cream
1 ounce chocolate
sugar

6 egg whites
vanilla

Add to the fresh cream only the best chocolate and sweeten to taste.

Have ready the egg whites beaten well and pour the chocolate cream over them. Stir thoroughly and quickly and strain through a sieve. Flavor with vanilla and serve cold.

COFFEE CREAM

1 ounce gelatine
½ cup strong aromatic coffee

½ cup sugar
1½ cups cream

Soak the gelatine in a little cold water for one-half hour. Place over boiling water and add the coffee and sugar.

When the gelatine is dissolved, take from the fire and stir in the cream. Pour the mixture into molds and allow to cool.

PINK CREAM

½ lb. powdered sugar
1½ cups strawberry juice
1 cup cream

Mix the sugar into the strawberry juice, add the cream and whisk until thoroughly mixed.

Serve in a glass dish.

LEMON CREAM

3 lemons
1 quart milk
6 eggs
2 cups sweetened water

Squeeze the juice of the lemons into the milk. Cut up the lemon peel, put it into the milk and cover. Let stand for an hour or two.

Beat the eggs very light and add them to the milk along with the sweetened water. Strain and simmer very slowly until thick, being careful not to boil.

Serve cold.

ORANGE CREAM

2 cups whipping cream
½ package gelatine
½ cup water
2 oranges
1 cup sugar
6 egg yolks
sweetened cream

Whip half the cream and set it aside.

Soak the gelatine in the cold water and grate into it the rind of both oranges. Mix in the sugar.

Put the remaining half of the cream into a double boiler and add the egg yolks, well-beaten. Stir constantly until the mixture begins to thicken, then add the gelatine.

Remove from the fire and let stand for a couple of minutes before adding the juice from the oranges. Beat all together until thick as boiled custard. Add the whipped cream, mix thoroughly and pour into molds to harden.

Serve with sweetened cream.

RUSSIAN CREAM

½ box gelatine
3 quarts milk
1 cup sugar
4 eggs
vanilla
cream

Dissolve the gelatine in part of the milk, then add the sugar and the egg yolks, well-beaten. Put in the rest of the milk, flavor with vanilla and heat until nearly boiling.

Remove from the fire and when quite cold, add the egg whites, well-beaten.

Pour into molds and serve with cream.

VELVET CREAM

This is a delicious dessert that can be made in a few minutes.

2 tablespoons gelatine
½ cup water
2 cups cream
4 tablespoons sugar
flavoring

Dissolve the gelatine in the water and add the cream and sugar. Flavor with sherry, vanilla or extract of rose water. Put on molds and set on ice.

Serve with or without cream.

WALNUT CREAM

3 egg yolks
2 cups milk
½ ounce gelatine
½ cup water
6 ounces powdered sugar
2 cups walnuts

wine
vanilla
cochineal [*or red food dye*]
2 cups whipping cream
a little egg white

Make a custard of the egg yolks and milk. Dissolve the gelatine in the water, mix in the powdered sugar and add to the custard when nearly cold.

Rub the nuts well in a coarse cloth to get rid of as much of the skins as possible. Pound to a paste with a little egg white.

Stir the walnut paste into the custard until smooth and fold in half of the whipped cream. Color a pale pink with cochineal and flavor with vanilla. Mold and set on ice.

Serve with the remainder of the whipped cream flavored with wine.

WHIPPED CREAM

3 egg whites
2 cups sweet cream
5 tablespoons sweet wine
3 tablespoons pulverized sugar
1 teaspoon lemon extract

Beat the egg white to a stiff froth and mix in the remaining ingredients. Whip until it stands solid.

Use a spoon to remove the froth as it rises and put it on an inverted sieve with a dish underneath to catch that which may drain through.

Whip again that which drains through.

BOILED CUSTARD

5 egg yolks
7 tablespoons sugar (1 for the meringue)
vanilla
1 quart milk
7 egg whites (2 for the meringue)

Beat the yolks very light, then stir in six tablespoons of sugar. Flavor with vanilla.

Heat the milk almost to boiling and remove from the fire. Add a couple of tablespoons at a time to the eggs and beat hard. As you beat, add more and more hot milk.

Whip solid the whites of five eggs and stir them into the mixture. Return to the fire and stir constantly until thick but not until it breaks. Pour into glass cups.

Whip the whites of two eggs to a meringue with one tablespoon of sugar. Pile upon each cup when the custard is cold. You may lay a little bright jelly upon the meringue, or a preserved cherry.

A GRAND TRIFLE

This is a delicious and highly ornamental dish but some trouble to prepare. It's not suitable for warm weather unless one has ice to keep all the parts in good order.

custard	**1 lb. almonds**
thin sponge cakes	**wine**
cream	**sugar**

The day before, make two or three quarts of boiled custard. You'll need plenty as the cake should stand in it all night and will soak it up.

Bake some thin sponge cakes.

Whip some cream with sugar and wine to flavor. Blanch and chop the almonds.

Place in a large glass bowl a layer of sponge cake, a thin layer of almonds, and a one-half-inch layer of whipped cream. Add another layer of cake, another of almonds and another of whipped cream. Cover with a third layer of cake.

Pour over all this plenty of custard. Put on more whipped cream as a float and decorate with pieces of red jelly and slender leaves of preserved orange peel.

Let stand overnight and serve.

ICE CREAM

2 eggs
14 ounces sugar
2 quarts cream
1 cup milk

First beat the eggs and sugar together as for cake. Then mix in the cream and milk. Put into the freezer and stir as it begins to freeze to make it perfectly smooth.

PURE ICE CREAM

If you desire rich ice cream, none but the purest article should be used. You cannot expect to make rich ice cream out of milk.

2 quarts pure sweet cream
1 lb. sugar

Combine the ingredients, beat up and freeze.

COFFEE ICE CREAM

14 ounces pulverized sugar
6 egg yolks

1 quart cream
2 cups strong coffee

Mix well sugar, egg yolks and cream. Put into the freezer.

When half frozen add the coffee, beat very hard and freeze.

TEA ICE CREAM

This makes quite a large quantity. One-fourth of the amount will suffice for a small family.

1 lb. sugar
2 cups strong green tea
3 cups cream

2 quarts milk
very little cinnamon water

Mix the ingredients and simmer for one minute. Do not stir but keep the mixture in motion by gently moving round the pan.

Freeze in the usual way.

LEMON ICE

4 lemons	**1 lb. sugar**
1 quart water	**3 egg whites**

Mix the juice of the lemons into the water. Dissolve in the sugar and strain.

When ready to freeze, beat the egg whites to a stiff froth and add.

WATER ICE

A few trials will enable you to make a syrup to your taste. Start with a syrup of a strength sufficient to bear up a fresh egg so a dime-size section shows above surface. You will soon learn how to vary it.

sugar	**fruit juice**
water	**egg whites**

Dissolve the sugar into the water to make a syrup of the proper sweetness.

Add fruit juice and the whites of eggs. Dilute and freeze.

PEACHES & CREAM

soft ripe peaches
sugar

powdered sugar
sweet cream

Peel the peaches and cut into quarters. Put a layer in a dish and sprinkle thick with sugar. Alternate in this way until the desired quantity is prepared.

Sprinkle a very heavy coat of powdered sugar on top of the fruit and set the dish on ice an hour or two before needed. Serve in small dishes poured over with rich sweet cream.

CHERRY SYRUP

6 lbs. cherries
6 cups hot water

3 lbs. sugar
1 egg white

Bruise the cherries, pour on the hot water and boil them for fifteen minutes. Strain through a flannel bag and add the sugar. Boil for another one-half hour or until a teaspoon of the liquid will sink to the bottom of a cup of water.

LEMON SHERBET

1 ¾ lbs. sugar
6 lemons
2 quarts boiling water

2 cups cream
5 egg whites

Mix the sugar with the juice of the lemons. Pour the boiling water over the rinds of the lemons and stir the water into the sugar and juice. Put the whole into the freezer.

When slightly frozen add the cream and egg whites beaten to a stiff froth and stirred well together.

MILK SHERBET

1 quart rich milk
sugar

vanilla
1 lemon

Sweeten the milk to suit your taste and flavor with vanilla. Freeze.

When nearly frozen, squeeze the juice of the lemon into the sherbet and stir well. Continue to freeze until solid.

FRIED PLANTAINS

plantains
sugar
butter

Peel and slice the plantains, sprinkle with sugar and fry them in very hot butter.

When done, sprinkle on more sugar and serve.

BAKED PLANTAINS

plantains
sugar
cinnamon
butter

Peel the plantains and place them in a baking dish, either whole or cut in squares. Sprinkle with sugar and cinnamon, and add a large lump of butter.

Baste several times while baking to prevent drying out.

199

BEVERAGES

SPRUCE BEER

1 ounce hops
1 tablespoon ginger
1 gallon water
2 cups molasses
½ ounce essence of spruce
½ cup yeast

This drink is flavored with essence of spruce which is an extract made from spruce twigs and leaves. —Mrs. B.

Adhering faithfully to the above proportions, stir the hops and ginger into the water and boil well. Then strain the liquid and add the molasses and the essence of spruce.

When cold, add the yeast and put it in a clean jug. Let it ferment for a day or two, then bottle it for use. You will find it good after three days.

CREAM BEER

A cool and refreshing beverage.

6 cups water
2 lemons
2¼ lbs. sugar
2 lbs. tartaric acid
3 egg whites
½ cup flour
½ ounce wintergreen essence
baking soda

Mix into the water the juice of the lemons, the sugar and the tartaric acid. Boil for five minutes.

When nearly cold add beaten egg whites, flour and wintergreen. Bottle and keep in a cool place.

To serve, use two tablespoons of syrup in a tumbler of cold water. Add one-quarter teaspoon of baking soda at the moment of consumption and shake the bottle before using.

TOMATO BEER

1 gallon tomato juice
3 lbs. brown sugar
sweetened water
essence of lemon

Mix together the tomato juice and sugar and let stand for nine days. Pour it off from the pulp which will settle to the bottom. Bottle closely. The longer you keep it the better it is.

To serve, take a pitcher of sweetened water and add a few drops of essence of lemon. For every quart, add one ounce of beer.

LEMONADE

Travelers may carry a box of lemon sugar prepared from citric acid and sugar. A spoon or two in a glass of cold water will furnish quite a refreshing drink and one that oftentimes averts headache and biliousness.

Citric acid is obtained from the juice of lemons and limes.

lemons
sugar

Roll the lemons until they become soft. Grate the rinds, cut the lemon in slices and squeeze them into a pitcher. Lacking a squeezer, a new clothespin will answer.

Pour in the required quantity of water and sweeten to taste. The grated rinds should be added for the sake of their aroma. After mixing thoroughly, set the pitcher aside for one-half hour.

Strain the liquor and add ice before serving.

LINSEED TEA

As an accessory it is in good repute and useful to allay irritation of the chest. Omitting the lemon, it is good for irritation of the lungs and gout.

1 tablespoon flax seed   **honey**
1 lemon   **orange peel**

Combine the ingredients in one quart of water and boil for ten minutes in a clean porcelain kettle. Sweeten with honey and add the juice of a lemon.

CHAMOMILE TEA

Drink a cupful half an hour before breakfast to promote digestion and restore the action of the liver. For an old person, a cupful in which has been stirred a teaspoon of sugar and a little ginger is an excellent tonic and stimulant when taken two hours before dinner.

30 chamomile flowers   **honey or sugar**
2 cups boiling water

Steep the chamomile flowers in the water and strain. Sweeten with honey or sugar.

ELDERBERRY WINE

4 quarts elderberries
1 gallon water
3 lbs. sugar
¼ ounce cream of tartar
¼ lb. raisins
1 slice of toast
yeast

Put the berries into the water and boil for one-half hour. Bruise from the skin and strain. Add the sugar and cream of tartar, and boil for another one-half hour.

Into a clean cask place the raisins and a slice of toasted bread covered with good yeast.

When the juice has cooled, pour it into the cask and place the cask in a room of even temperature to ferment.

When fermentation has fully ceased, put the bung in tight. No brandy or alcohol should be added.

UNFERMENTED WINE

1 gallon pure grape juice
1 lb. sugar

Mix the grape juice and the sugar together in a porcelain kettle and boil gently, skimming carefully.

Simmer slowly until the liquid is reduced to about one-fifth the original quantity.

Bottle while hot and you will have a rich, refreshing drink.